Classical Text-Book Series.

FIRST ORATION

OF

CICERO AGAINST CATILINE

WITH

NOTICES, NOTES AND COMPLETE VOCABULARY.

BY

JOHN HENDERSON, M. A.

HEAD MASTER, COLLEGIATE INSTITUTE, ST. CATHARINES.

TORONTO:

THE COPP, CLARK COMPANY, LIMITED,

9 FRONT STREET WEST.

1886.

PREFACE.

It has been the aim of the Editor to explain what seemed to him difficulties in the text. There are many points which might have been noted, but which a judicious teacher will supply in the ordinary class work.

References are made to the standard grammars of Zumpt, Madvig, Harkness, Allen and Greenough.

St. Catharines, September, 1886.

LIFE OF CICERO.

I.

Marcus Tullius Cicero,[1] the greatest name *Birth.*
in Roman literature, was born near Arpinum, a town
of Latium, January 3rd, B.C. 106. His father, a
man of large views and liberal culture, belonged to
the *equites*, and possessed an hereditary estate in the
neighbourhood of the town. To give his sons, Marcus and Quintus, that education which could not be
obtained at a provincial school, he removed to Rome, *Removes to*
where the young Ciceros were placed under the best *Rome,*
B.C. 92.
teachers of the day. From Aelius they learned
philosophy; from Archias, the mechanism of verse, *Early*
though not the inspiration of poetry. A translation *teachers.*
of the *Phaenomena* and *Prognostics* of Aratus, and a *Early works.*
mythological poem on the fable of *Pontius Glaucus*
were the first fruits of Cicero's genius. On assuming *Assumes the*
the *toga virilis*, B.C. 89, Cicero attached himself to *toga virilis*
B.C. 89.
the jurist Scaevola, who was then in the zenith of his
fame. In the following year he served a brief cam- *Serves his*
paign in the Social War under Cn. Pompeius Strabo, *first cam-*
paign,
the father of Pompey the Great. Philosophical *B.C. 88.*
studies had, however, more attractions for him than
arms. Under Philo, the Academic, and Diodotus, *Studies*
the Stoic, he laid the foundation of that Eclecticism *philosophy.*
which is so observable in his philosophical works.
At the age of 25 he pleaded his first cause, and in *Pleads his*
the following year he defended Sextus Roscius of *first cause*
pro Quinct
Ameria, who had been accused of parricide by Chry-
sogonus, one of Sylla's favourites. In this cause he

acquired the acquittal of his client, but incurred the enmity of the dictator. With the ostensible object *Goes to Athens, Asia, and Rhodes.* of regaining his health he went to Athens, where he studied philosophy under Antiochus, the Academic, and under Zeno and Phaedrus, both Epicureans. From Athens he travelled through Asia Minor and finally settled for a short time at Rhodes, attending *Returns home.* there the lectures of Molo, the rhetorician. Return- ing home, he at once entered on that political career to which his commanding ability destined him, and *Elected quaestor of Sicily* was elected *quaestor* of Sicily. During his term of office he so endeared himself to the inhabitants of the island by his integrity that they selected him as their patron at Rome. In their behalf he subsequently *Indicts Verres, B.C. 70.* conducted the prosecution against Verres, who was charged with extortion. His success in this cause, and his consequent popularity, procured him the *Elected aedile, 69 B.C.* office of *curule aedile.* After the usual interval he *Praetor, 66 B.C.* was chosen *praetor*, and, while holding this office, delivered the first of his political harangues, in de- *His first political speech.* fence of the bill proposed by C. Manilius to invest Pompey with supreme command in the Mithradatic *Pro lege Manilia, 65 B.C.* War. Two years afterwards he gained the *consul-* *Consul, 63 B.C.* ship, the goal of his ambition. His consulate is memorable for the bold attempt of Catiline to sub- vert the government—an attempt which was frus- *Unpopu- larity of Cicero.* trated by the patriotic zeal of the consul. Cicero had quickly soared to the pinnacle of fame : as quickly did he fall. In crushing the conspiracy of Catiline questionable means had been employed. Clodius, *Causes of Exile.* his implacable enemy, revived a law exiling all who had been guilty of putting to death Roman citizens without a formal trial before the people. The *Deserted by the Triumvirs.* Triumvirs, too, were disgusted with the vanity of the man who was constantly reminding the people that he was the "Saviour of Italy" and the "Father of

His Country." Deserted by his friends, and exposed to the hatred of his foes, Cicero went to Thessalonica into voluntary exile. The wanton destruction of his *Goes into exile,* *58 B.C.* villas and the insults offered to his wife and children soon, however, produced a feeling of sympathy for the exiled orator. His return to Rome was attended *Recall,* *51 B.C.* with all the pomp and circumstance of a triumphant general. Henceforth his voice was little heard in the Senate. After his return he was appointed to a seat *Elected Augur,* *53 B.C.* in the *College of Augurs.* In obtaining this office he had placed himself under obligations to both Pompey and Caesar, and this may account for his neutrality in the civil struggles of the time. He was subse- quently appointed, much against his will, proconsul *Proconsul,* *52 B.C.* of Cilicia, where his administration was marked by the same integrity as he had displayed in Sicily. Cicero arrived in Italy from Cilicia on the 4th of January, B.C. 49, just after the breaking out of the civil war between Pompey and Caesar. After some hesitation he decided to take the part of Pompey, *Sides with Pompey.* but his support was never cordial : it was a source of weakness rather than of strength. When the battle of Pharsalia decided the fate of the Roman world, he *Pharsalia, B.C. 48.* returned to Brundisium to await the arrival of the victorious Caesar, who generously extended a full and frank pardon to the vacillating orator. Cicero *Pardoned by Caesar.* from this time withdrew from active public life and devoted himself to philosophy, except during the period immediately preceding his death. The loss of his daughter Tullia, the divorce of his wife Terentia, and the unhappy marriage with Publilia darkened the gloom which settled on his declining years. His *Gloom.* high exultation on the assassination of Caesar was of only momentary duration, and was succeeded by dark forebodings of Marc Anthony's designs. As soon as the plans of the scheming triumvir were evident,

His
Philippic
Orations.
Cicero attacked Antony's character with all the powers of invective. Again he was the idol of the people and the champion of senatorial rights, but his popularity was only the last gasp of the dying liberties of Rome. The second triumvirate

Antony,
Octavianus,
and Sepidus
form the
second
triumvirate.
was formed, and each member of it sacrificed his friends to glut the vengeance of his colleagues ; and to appease the brutal Antony, Cicero was sacrificed by Octavianus. Refusing to seek refuge in exile, he

Killed at
Caieta,
B.C. 43.
determined to die in the land he had saved, and was slain at Caieta by the emissaries of the bloodthirsty triumvir.

Works.
The works of Circero are : —

(1) *Orations :* Of the eighty speeches composed by him we possess, either entire or in part, fifty-nine. (See list).

(2) *Philosophical works.*

(3) *Correspondence :* Comprising *thirty-six* books, *sixteen* of which are addressed to Athens, *three* to his brother Quintus, *one* to Brutus, and *sixteen* to his different friends.

(4) *Poems :* Consisting of the heroic poems, *Alcyones, Marcus, Elegy of Tamelastis,* and *Translations* of Homer and Aratus.

II.

LIFE OF CATILINE.

Birth.
L. Sergius Catilina w. ~ a Roman patrician, born about 108 B.C. From his father he inherited nothing but a noble name. In the turbulent scenes of the Sullan rule, Catiline played a conspicuous part, to which his undoubted ability, his undaunted courage, his iron constitution, his depraved morals, and excessive cruelty notoriously fitted him. He

commenced his career by slaying, with his own hand, *His crimes.*
Q. Caecilius, his own brother-in-law, and by torturing
to death M. Marius Gratidianus, a kinsman of Cicero.
Though his youth was spent in open debauchery, and
reckless extravagance, though he made away with
his first wife and his son to marry the worthless and
profligate Aurelia Orestilla, the guilty crimes of
Catiline do not seem to have been any barrier to his
advancement to political honors.   He obtained the
praetorship B.C. 68, and in the following year was *Offices held.*
propraetor of Africa.   He returned to Rome B.C. 66
to press his suit for the consulship.   The two consuls
who had the highest votes were P. Autronius Paetus
and P. Cornelius Sulla, both of whom were convicted
of bribery, and their election was declared void.
Their places were filled by L. Aurelius Cotta and L.
Manlius Torquatus.   Catiline was prevented from
being a candidate in consequence of an impeachment
brought against him for mal-administration of his
province of Africa by P. Clodius Pulcher, afterwards
the implacable enemy of Cicero.   Autronius and
Catiline, exasperated by their disappointment, formed
a league with Cn. Calpurnius Piso to murder the
consuls on the first of January, to seize the *fasces,* *First*
and to occupy Spain.   The plan leaked out, and was *Conspiracy.*
postponed till the fifth of February.   The scheme,
however, failed in consequence of Catiline giving the
signal too soon.   Resolutions were passed by the
Senate condemning the conspiracy, but these were
quashed by the intercession of a tribune.   Some say
that both Caesar and Crassus were involved in this
First Conspiracy of Catiline.   About this time,
Catiline was acquitted of extortion *(res repetundae),*
but the trial rendered him penniless.   About the
beginning of June, 64 B.C., he began to plot more
systematically to carry out his plans for a general

revolution. A meeting was called for all those interested in the conspiracy. To this convention, eleven senators, four knights, and many of the noted men from the provincial towns assembled to hear the *Catiline's* bold designs of the conspirator. Catiline proposed *Proposals.* that all debts should be cancelled *(novae tabulae),* that the wealthy citizens should be proscribed, that offices of honor and emolument should be divided among his friends, and that the leaders of the conspiracy should raise armies in Spain and in Mauretania. Again he was a candidate for the consulship, and again he was doomed to disappointment. Cicero and Antonius were chosen, the latter, however, by only a few centuries over Catiline. This defeat embittered the animosity between the two parties. The conspirator raised large sums of money on his own security and on the credit of his friends, sent arms to various parts of Italy, levied troops in Etruria, and sent Manlius a veteran of Sulla to take command of the newly raised forces. The slaves were to be armed, the buildings of the city set on fire, the citizens indiscriminately massacred, and a reign of terror and bloodshed was to be inaugurated. In the midst of all these schemes, Catiline stood again for the consulship (63 B.C.), and was thwarted by the wariness and exertions of Cicero, who checkmated his schemes at every turn. One of the conspirators was Q. Curius, a man weak and vacillating. This man had a mistress, Fulvia, who was *The Con-* the repository of all his secrets. Alarmed at the *spiracy* *divulged.* audacious designs of the conspirators, she imparted her secrets to some of her acquaintances, and through her confidants the matter was betrayed to Cicero. After securing his personal safety, and withdrawing Antonius from the side of Catiline, the consul deferred the consular elections to lay before the Senate the whole conspiracy. At a meeting of the Senate, *First Speech* October 21st, 63, he told the Senators the danger *against Catiline.* that threatened the state. Many of those complicated in the conspiracy fled. By virtue of a *decretum ultimum*, which formula *(consules videant, ne quid detrimenti respublica capiat)* gave the consuls absolute civil and military power, Catiline was in danger of losing his life. Catiline, who was again a candidate for the consulship for 62 B.C., was rejected. An impeachment of sedition was also brought against him by L. Aemilius Paulus. On the 6th November, Catiline summoned the conspirators to the house of M. Porcius Laeca, and after accusing them of inactivity, he laid before him his plans. Cicero was to be removed, and L. Vargunteius, a senator, and C. Cornelius, a knight, were despatched to carry out the scheme, but were frustrated. Cicero called the Senate on November 8th, and delivered his first speech against Catiline, who, though overwhelmed with guilt, had still the audacity to appear among the senators.

Altogether four speeches were delivered against Catiline. In the final debate as to the sentence, it was decided to put the apprehended conspirators to death. This sentence was carried out against some. Catiline and most fell, however, in the field at Pistoria (62 B.C.), fighting with a valour worthy of a better cause.

III.

CHRONOLOGY OF THE CONSPIRACY OF CATILINE.

DATE.	CONSULS.	LIFE OF CATILINE.	LIFE OF CICERO.
B.C. 68	{ L. Caecilius Metellus P. Marcus Rex	Catiline praetor	
67	{ Calpurnius Piso M. Acilius Glabrio	Catiline propraetor of Africa	
66	{ L. Volcatius Tullus M. Aemilius Lepidus	Catiline canvasses for the consulship: is accused of extortion by P. Clodius. Catiline defeated in suing for consulship: forms a league with Autronius and Piso. First conspiracy.	
65	{ L. Manlius Torquatus L. Aurelius Cotta	Catiline determines to slay the new consuls on the kalends of January: plan discovered and deferred to February: Catiline gives signal too soon and his plans frustrated.	
64	{ L. Julius Caesar C. Marcus Figulus	On the kalends of June, Catiline convenes his associates for a second conspiracy. Eleven senators, four knights, and many distinguished men assemble. Catiline again defeated for consulship.	
63	{ M. Tullius Cicero C. Antonius Hybrida	Catiline accused by Lucullus of murder. Catiline again candidate for consulship and defeated.	Cicero convenes Senate, Oct. 20: lays plans of conspirators before Senate: elections for consuls, which should take place Oct. 21st, deferred.

CHRONOLOGY, &c.—(Continued).

DATE.	CONSULS.	LIFE OF CATILINE.	LIFE OF CICERO.
B.C. 63		Oct. 23rd : Catiline accused under *Lex Plautia de vi* by Lucius Paulus. Oct. 27th : Manlius takes up arms in Etruria. Oct. 28th : Day appointed by Catiline for the murder of the leading senators. (Cat. I., 3). Nov. 1 : Catiline endeavors to take Praeneste by a night attack. Nov. 6th : Catiline assembles his friends at house of Laeca. Nov. 7th : Vargunteius and Cornelius attempt to assassinate Cicero. Nov. 8th : Catiline leaves Rome. Nov. 20th : A decree passed declaring Catiline and Manlius public enemies. Dec. 2nd : The ambassadors of the Allobroges are seized with documents proving conspiracy.	Oct. 21st : Letters brought by Crassus, threatening danger to the State : the Senate convened in the temple of Concord. The Senate passes *decretum ultimum.* On 22nd Oct. L. Licinius Murena and D. Junius Silanus elected consuls. Nov. 8 : Cicero invokes the Senate in the temple of Juppiter Stator. First Catilinarian oration delivered. The *second Catilinarian oration* delivered from the *rostra* to the people, Nov. 9th. Dec. 3rd : The *third Catilinarian oration* delivered from the rostra to the people. Rewards offered to all who would give information as to the conspiracy.

CHRONOLOGY, &c.—*(Continued)*.

DATE.	CONSULS.	LIFE OF CATILINE.	LIFE OF CICERO.
B.C.			Dec. 5th : Fourth Catilinarian oration delivered in the temple of Concord. The Senate decrees that the death penalty should be inflicted on the conspirators. Five conspirators put to death.
62	D. Junius Silanus L. Licinius Murena	Jan. 5th: Battle of *Pistoria*: defeat and death of Catiline.	Many Senators tried under the law *Lex Plautia de vi* and exiled.

IV.

FIRST ORATION AGAINST CATILINE.

This speech may be divided into three parts :

I. In the introduction Cicero in impassioned language expresses astonishment that Catiline should be so audacious as to come into the Senate while plotting the destruction of his country. The orator reminds Catiline that men less guilty have been slain in the earlier days of the republic, and gives reasons why the penalty of death should be meted out to the arch conspirator (I., II.).

II. In the next part, Cicero gives reasons why Catiline should leave Rome and go to the camp of Manlius :

    (*a*) That his nefarious plot was well known, that his personal character was stained with many crimes, that his public life was abhorred by all, that his native land, though silent, eloquently pleads with Catiline to withdraw (III.-IX.).

(*b*) That Catiline should depart to the troops raised in Etruria, whither he had sent Manlius to carry on the war, that the great delight of Catiline was to make war on his native land, and to mingle in the society of the conspirators.

(*c*) That such withdrawal would be more advantageous to the State than the execution of the conspirators, that in the former case his abandoned followers would accompany Catiline, and thus the seeds of the rebellion would be extirpated.

III. The orator promises the co-operation of all patriotic citizens in suppressing the conspiracy after Catiline and his associates had withdrawn. Then beseeching Catiline and the other conspirators to remove from Rome, the orator invokes the aid of Juppiter Stator to save Rome from the nefarious schemes of abandoned men.

M. TULLII CICERONIS

ORATIO IN L. CATILINAM

PRIMA.

HABITA IN SENATU.

I.—1. ¹Quo ūsque tandem abūtēre, Catilina, patientia nostra? Quam diu ²etiam ³furor iste tuus ⁴eludet? ⁵Quem ad finem sese effrenata ⁶jactabit audacia? ⁷Nihilne te nocturnum praesidium Palatii, nihil urbis vigiliae, nihil timor populi, nihil concursus bonorum omnium, nihil hic munitissimus habendi senatus locus, nihil horum ora vultusque moverunt? Patēre tua consilia non sentis? ⁸Constrictam omnium horum scientia teneri conjurationem tuam non vides? Quid ⁹proxima, quid superiore nocte ēgeris, ubi fueris, quos convocaveris, quid consilii ceperis, quem ¹⁰nostrum ignorare arbitraris? 2. O tempora, O mores! senatus haec intellegit, consul videt: hic tamen vivit.¹ Vivit? immo vero etiam ²in senatum venit, fit publici consilii particeps, ⁸notat et designat oculis ad caedem unum quemque nostrum./ Nos autem, ⁴viri fortes, satis facere rei publicae ⁵videmur, si istīus furorem ac tela ⁶vitemus. ⁷Ad mortem te, Catilina, duci jussu consulis iam pridem oportebat, ⁸in te conferri pestem istam, quam tu in nos machinaris. 3. ¹An vero vir amplissimus, P. Scipio, pontifex maximus, Ti. Gracchum, mediocriter labefactantem statum rei publicae, privatus interfecit: Catilinam orbem terrae caede atque incendiis vastare cupientem, nos consules perferemus? Nam ²illa nimis

2

antiqua praetereo, quod C. [3]Servilius Ahala Sp. Maelium,
[4]novis rebus studentem, manu sua occidit. [5]Fuit, fuit ista
quondam in hac re publica virtus, [6]ut viri fortes acerbiori-
bus suppliciis civem perniciosum quam acerbissimum
hostem coercerent. Habemus [7]senatus consultum in te,
Catilina, [8]vehemens et grave : non deest [9]rei publicae
consilium neque auctoritas hujus ordinis : [10]nos, nos, dico
aperte, consules desumus.

II.—4. Decrevit [1]quondam senatus ut L. Opimius consul videret ne quid res publica detrimenti caperet ; nox
nulla [2]intercessit ; interfectus est [3]propter quasdam sedi-
tionum suspiciones C. Gracchus, clarissimo [4]patre, avo,
majoribus : occisus est cum liberis[5] M. Fulvius consularis.
[6]Simili senatus consulto C. Mario et L. Valerio consulibus
est permissa res publica : [7]num unum diem postea L.
Saturninum tribunum plebis et C. Servilium praetorem
mors ac rei publicae poena remorata est? At vero nos
[8]vicesimum jam diem patimur hebescere [9]aciem horum
auctoritatis. Habemus enim hujus modi senatus consultum, verum [10]inclusum in tabulis tamquam in vagina recon-
ditum,[11] quo ex senatus consulto confestim interfectum te
esse, Catilina, convenit. Vivis, [12]et vivis non ad deponen-
dam sed ad confirmandam audaciam. Cupio, patres
conscripti, me esse clementem, cupio in tantis rei publicae
periculis me non [13]dissolutum videri, sed jam me ipse
[13]inertiae nequitiaeque condemno. 5. [1]Castra sunt in Italia
contra populum Romanum in Etruriae faucibus collocata,
crescit [2]in dies singulos hostium numerus, eorum autem
castorum imperatorem ducemque hostium intra moenia
atque [3]adeo in senatu videmus intestinam aliquam cotidie
perniciem rei publicae molientem. Si te [4]jam, Catilina,
comprehendi, si interfici jussero, [5]credo, erit [6]verendum
mihi, ne non potius hoc omnes boni serius a me quam
quisquam crudelius factum esse dicat. Verum ego hoc,

quod jam pridem factum esse oportuit, [7]certa de causa
nondum adducor, ut faciam.   Tum denique [8]interficiĕre,
cum jam nemo tam improbus, tam perditus, tam [9]tui
similis inveniri poterit, [10]qui id nonjure factum esse fateatur.
6. Quam diu [1]quisquam erit qui te defendere audeat, vives,
sed vives ita, ut [2]vivis, multis meis et firmis praesidiis
oppressus, ne [3]commovere te contra rem publicam possis.
Multorum te etiam oculi et aures non sentientem, sicut
adhuc [4]fecerunt, speculabuntur atque custodient.

III.—[5]Etenim quid est, Catilina, quod jam amplius [6]ex-
spectes, si neque nox tenebris obscurare [7]coeptus nefarios
neque [8]privata domus [9]parietibus continere [10]voces conjurationis tuae potest ?   Si [11]inlustrantur, si erumpunt omnia ?
Muta jam [12]istam mentem, [13]mihi crede ! obliviscere caedis
atque incendiorum.   [14]Teneris undique luce sunt clariora
nobis tua consilia omnia ; quae jam mecum licet [15]reco-
gnoscas.   7. [1]Meministine me [2]ante diem duodecimum
Kalendas Novembres dicere in senatu, fore in armis [3]certo
die, qui dies futurus esset ante diem sextum Kalendas
Novembres, C. Manlium, [4]audaciae satellitem atque ad-
ministrum tuae ?   [5]Num me fefellit, Catilina, non modo
res tanta, tam atrox, tamque incredibilis, verum id quod
multo magis admirandum, dies? Dixi ego idem in senatu,
[6]caedem te [7]optimatium contulisse in ante diem quintum
Kalendas Novembres, tum cum multi principes civitatis
Roma non tam [8]sui conservandi quam tuorum consiliorum
[9]reprimendorum causa profugerunt.   Num infitiari potes
te illo die meis praesidiis, mea diligentia circumclusum
commovere te contra rem publicam non potuisse, cum tu
discessu ceterorum nostra tamen, qui remansissemus,
caede contentum se dicebas ? 8. [1]Quid ? cum tu [2]te Praeneste Kalendis ipsis Novembribus occupaturum nocturno
impetu esse confideres, [3]sensistine illam coloniam meo
jussu meis praesidiis, custodiis vigiliisque esse munitam ?

⁵Nihil agis, nihil moliris, nihil cogitas, quod non ego non modo audiam, sed etiam videam planeque sentiam.

IV.—Recognosce mecum ⁶tandem ⁷noctem illam superiorem : ⁸jam intelliges multo me vigilare acrius ad salutem quam te ad perniciem rei publicae. ⁹Dico te ¹⁰priore nocte venisse ¹¹inter falcarios—non agam obscure ¹²in M. Laecae domum: convenisse eodem ¹³complures ejusdem ¹⁴amentiae scelerisque socios. Num negare audes ? quid taces ? ¹⁵convincam, si negas : video enim esse hic in senatu quosdam, qui tecum una fuerunt. 9. O di immortales ! ¹ubinam gentium sumus ! quam rem publicam habemus ? in qua urbe vivimus ? ²Hic, hic sunt in nostro numero, ³patres conscripti, ⁴in hoc orbis terrae sanctissimo gravissimoque consilio, ⁵qui de nostro omnium interitu, qui de hujus urbis atque adeo de orbis terrarum exitio cogitent. Hosce ego video et de re publica ⁶sententiam rogo, quos ferro trucidari oportebat, eos nondum voce ⁷vulnero. Fuisti ⁸igitur apud Laecam illa nocte, Catilina ; ⁹distribuisti partes Italiae ; ¹⁰statuisti quo quemque proficisci placeret; ¹¹delegisti quos Romae relinqueres, quos tecum educeres; ¹²discripsisti urbis partes ad incendia; confirmasti te ipsum jam esse exiturum; dixisti ¹³paullulum tibi esse ¹⁴etiam tum morae, quod ego viverem. Reperti sunt ¹⁵duo equites Romani, ¹⁶qui te ista cura liberarent et sese illa ipsa nocte paulo ante lucem me in meo ¹⁷lectulo interfecturos esse pollicerentur. 10. Haec ego omnia, ¹vixdum etiam coetu vestro dimisso, comperi, domum meam majoribus praesidiis munivi atque firmavi, exclusi eos, quos tu ad me ²salutatum ³mane miseras, cum illi ipsi venissent, quos ego jam multis ac summis viris ad me ⁴id temporis venturos praedixeram.

V.—11. ¹Quae cum ita sint, Catilina, ²perge quo coepisti, egredĕre aliquando ex urbe : patent portae : proficiscĕre.

Nimium diu te imperatorem tua illa Manliana castra desiderant. Educ tecum etiam omnes tuos, ³si minus, quam plurimos : purga urbem. Magno me metu liberabis, ⁴dum modo inter me atque te murus intersit.   Nobiscum versari jam diutius non potes : ⁵non feram, non patiar, non sinam.   ⁶Magna dis immortalibus habenda est atque huic ipsi Jovi Statori, antiquissimo custodi hujus urbis, gratia, ⁷quod hanc tam taetram, tam horribilem tamque infestam rei publicae pestem totiens jam effugimus.   ⁹Non est saepius in uno homine summa salus periclitanda rei publicae. Quam diu mihi, ⁸consuli designato, Catilina, insidiatus es, non publico me praesidio, sed privata diligentia defendi. | Cum, proximis comitiis consularibus, me consulem ¹⁰in campo et ¹¹competitores tuos interficere voluisti, ¹²compressi conatus tuos nefarios amicorum praesidio et copiis, nullo tumultu publice concitato : denique, ¹³quotiens-cumque me petisti, per me tibi obstiti, ¹⁴quamquam vide-bam ¹⁵perniciem meam cum magna calamitate rei publicae esse conjunctam.   12. ¹Nunc jam aperte rem publicam universam petis : templa deorum immortalium, tecta urbis, vitam omnium civium, Italiam ²denique totam ad exitium ac vastitatem vocas.   ³Quare quoniam id, quod est primum et quod hujus imperii disciplinaeque majorum proprium est, facere nondum audeo, faciam id, quod est ⁴ad severitatem lenius et ad communem salutem utilius. Nam si te interfici jussero, residebit in re publica ⁵reliqua conjuratorum manus : ⁶sin tu, quod te jam dudum hortor, exieris, ⁷exhaurietur ex urbe tuorum comitum magna et perniciosa reipublicae.   13. Quid est, Catilina ? num dubitas id ¹imperante me facere, quod jam tua sponte ²faciebas ? Exire ex urbe jubet ³consul hostem.   Interro-gas me : ⁴num in exilium ? non jubeo, sed, si ⁵me consulis, suadeo.

VI.—Quid est enim, Catilina, ⁶quod te jam in hac urbe delectare possit? In qua nemo est ⁷extra istam conjurationem perditorum hominum qui te non metuat, nemo qui non oderit. ⁸Quae nota domesticae turpitudinis non inusta vitae tuae est? ⁹Quod privatarum rerum dedecus non haeret in fama?—¹⁰Quae libido ab oculis, quod facinus a manibus unquam tuis, quod flagitium a toto corpore abfuit? ¹¹Cui tu adulescentulo, quem corruptelarum illecebris irretisses, non aut ad audaciam ferrum aut ad libidinem facem praetulisti? 14. ¹Quid vero? ²Nuper, cum morte superioris uxoris novis nuptiis domum vacuefecisses, nonne etiam alio incredibili scelere hoc scelus cumulasti? Quod ego praetermitto et facile ³patior sileri, ne in hac civitate ⁴tanti facinoris immanitas, aut exstitisse aut non vindicata esse videatur. Praetermitto ruinas fortunarum tuarum, ⁵quas omnes impendere tibi proximis Idibus senties : ad illa venio, quae non ad privatam ignominiam vitiorum tuorum, non ad domesticam tuam difficultatem ac turpitudinem, sed ad summam rem publicam atque ⁶ad omnium nostrum vitam salutemque pertinent. 15. Potestne tibi haec lux, Catilina, aut hujus caeli spiritus esse jucundus, ¹cum scias esse horum ²neminem qui nesciat, te ³pridie Kalendas Januarias ⁴Lepido et Tullo Consulibus stetisse in ⁵comitio cum telo? Manum consulum et principum civitatis interficiendorum causa paravisse ⁶sceleri ac furori tuo non mentem aliquam aut timorem tuum, sed fortunam populi Romani obstitisse? Ac jam illa omitto—⁷neque enim sunt aut obscura aut non multa commissa postea :—quotiens tu me ⁸designatum, quotiens consulem interficere voluisti! quot ego tuas ⁹petitiones ¹⁰ita conjectas, ut vitari posse non viderentur, parva quadam declinatione et, ut aiunt, corpore effugi! nihil adsequeris, neque tamen conari ac velle desistis. 16. Quotiens ¹tibi jam extorta est sica ista de manibus! quotiens ²excidit *et eos*

aliquo casu et elapsa est! ³quae quidem quibus abs te
initiata sacris ac devota sit, nescio, quod eam necesse
putas esse in consulis corpore defigere.

∧ VII.—Nunc vero quae ⁴tua est ista vita? Sic enim jam
tecum loquar, non ut odio permotus esse videar, quo
debeo, ⁵sed ut misericordia, quae tibi ⁶nulla debetur.
Venisti ⁷paulo ante in senatum. Quis te ex hac tanta
frequentia, tot ex tuis amicis ac necessariis salutavit? Si
hoc ⁹post hominum memoriam contigit nemini, ¹⁰vocis
exspectas contumeliam, cum sis gravissimo judicio taciturnitatis oppressus? ¹¹Quid? Quod ¹²adventu tuo ¹³ista
subsellia vacuefacta sunt, quod omnes consulares, ¹⁴qui
tibi persaepe ad caedem constituti fuerunt, simul atque ad-
sedisti, partem istam subselliorum ¹⁵nudam atque inanem
reliquerunt, quo ¹⁶tandem animo hoc tibi ferendum putas?
17. ¹Servi ²mehercule mei si me ³isto pacto metuerent, ut
te metuunt omnes cives tui, domum meam relinquendam
putarem: tu tibi ⁴urbem non arbitraris? Etsi me meis
civibus ⁵injuria suspectum tam graviter atque ⁶offensum
viderem, carere me aspectu civium quam ⁷infestis oculis
omnium conspici mallem: tu cum conscientia scelerum
tuorum ⁷agnoscas odium omnium justum et jam diu tibi
debitum, ⁹dubitas, quorum ¹⁰mentes sensusque vulneras,
eorum aspectum praesentiamque vitare? Si te parentes
timerent atque odissent tui nec eos ulla ratione placare
posses, ut, opinor, ab eorum oculis ¹¹aliquo concederes:
¹²nunc te patria ¹³quae communis est parens omnium nostrum, odit ac metuit et jam diu nihil te judicat nisi de parricidio suo cogitare: hujus tu neque auctoritatem ¹⁴vere-
bere nec judicium sequere nec vim pertimesces? 18. ¹Quae
tecum, Catilina, sic agit et quodam modo tacita loquitur:
²ᵗNullum jam aliquot annis facinus exstitit nisi per te, nullum flagitium sine te: tibi uni multorum civium ³neces,
tibi vexatio direptioque ⁴sociorum impunita fuit ac libera:

[5]tu non solum ad negligendas leges et quaestiones, verum etiam ad evertendas perfringendasque valuisti. Superiora illa, quamquam ferenda non fuerunt, tamen ut potui, tuli : nunc vero me totam esse in metu propter unum te, quidquid increpuerit Catilinam timeri, nullum videri contra me consilium iniri posse, quod a tuo scelere abhorreat, [6]non est ferendum. Quamobrem discede atque hunc mihi timorem eripe, si est verus, [6]ne opprimar, sin falsus, ut tandem aliquando timere desinam.'

VIII.—19. Haec si tecum, ut dixi, patria loquatur, nonne [1]impetrare debeat, etiam si vim adhibere non possit? [2]Quid? Quod tu te ipse [3]in custodiam dedisti? Quod vitandae suspicionis causa [4]apud M'. Lepidum te habitare velle dixisti? A quo non receptus etiam ad me venire ausus es, atque ut domi meae te adservarem rogasti. Cum a me quoque id responsum tulisses, me nullo modo posse [5]isdem parietibus tuto esse tecum, qui magno in periculo essem quod isdem moenibus contineremur, ad [6]Q. Metellum praetorem venisti : a quo repudiatus ad sodalem tuum, [7]virum optimum, M. Metellum demigrasti, quem tu [8]videlicet et ad custodiendum diligentissimum et ad suspicandum sagacissimum et [9]ad vindicandum fortissimum fore putasti. Sed quam longe videtur a carcere atque vinculis abesse debere, [10]qui se ipse jam dignum custodia judicarit? | 20. [1]Quae cum ita sint, dubitas, si [2]emori aequo animo non potes, abire in aliquas terras et vitam istam, multis suppliciis justis debitisque ereptam, fugae solitudinique mandare ? [3]Refer, inquis, ad senatum ; id enim postulas, et, si hic ordo [4]sibi placere decreverit te ire in exilium, obtemperaturum te esse dicis. Non referam, id quod [5]abhorret a meis moribus, et tamen faciam ut intelligas, quid hi de te sentiant. Egredere ex urbe, Catilina, libera rem publicam metu, in exilium, [6]si hanc vocem exspectas, proficiscere. Quid est, Catilina?

Ecquid attendis, ecquid animadvertis horum silentium? [7]Patiuntur, tacent. [8]Quid exspectas auctoritatem loquentium, quorum voluntatem tacitorum perspicis? 21. At si hoc idem [1]huic adulescenti optimo, P. Sestio, si fortissimo viro M. Marcello dixissem, jam mihi consuli hoc ipso in templo jure optimo senatus [2]vim et manus intulisset. De te autem, Catilina, cum [3]quiescunt, probant, cum patiuntur, decernunt, cum tacent, clamant : neque hi solum, quorum auctoritas est videlicet cara, vita vilissima, sed etiam equites Romani honestissimi atque optimi viri, ceterique fortissimi [4]cives, qui stant circum senatum, quorum tu et frequentiam videre et studia perspicere et voces paulo ante exaudire potuisti. Quorum ego vix abs te jam diu manus ac tela contineo, eosdem facile adducam ut te haec, quae jam pridem vastare studes, relinquentem usque ad portas [6]prosequantur.

IX.—22. [1]Quamquam quid loquor? Te ut ulla res frangat? Tu ut te unquam corrigas? Tu ut ullam fugam meditere? Tu ut exilium cogites? Utinam tibi istam mentem di immortales [3]duint! Etsi video, si mea voce perterritus ire in exilium [4]animum induxeris, [5]quanta tempestas invidiae nobis, si minus in praesens tempus, recenti memoria scelerum tuorum, at in posteritatem impendeat. Sed est tanti, dum modo ista sit privata calamitas, et a rei publicae periculis sejungatur. Sed tu [7]ut vitiis commoveare, ut legum poenas pertimescas, ut temporibus rei publicae cedas, non est postulandum. Neque enim is es, Catilina, ut te aut pudor unquam a turpitudine aut metus a periculo aut ratio a furore revocaverit. 23. Quam ob rem, ut saepe jam dixi, proficiscere, ac, si mihi inimico, ut praedicas, tuo [1]conflare vis invidiam, [2]recta perge in exilium ; [3]vix feram sermones hominum, si id feceris, vix molem istius invidiae, si in exilium jussu consulis ieris, sustinebo. [4]Sin autem servire meae laudi et gloriae

mavis, egredere cum importuna sceleratorum manu.
Confer te ad Manlium, concita perditos cives, secernc
te a bonis, infer patriae bellum, [5]exsulta impio latrocinio,
ut a me non ejectus ad alienos, sed invitatus ad tuos esse
videaris. 24. [1]Quamquam quid ego te invitem, a quo
jam sciam esse praemissos, [2]qui tibi ad Forum Aurelium
praestolarentur armati? Cui sciam [3]pactam et consti-
tutam cum Manlio diem. A quo etiam [4]aquilam illam
argenteam, quam tibi ac tuis omnibus perniciosam esse
confido ac funestam futuram, [6]cui domi tuae sacrarium
scelerum tuorum constitutum fuit, sciam esse praemis-
sam? [6]Tu ut illa diutius carere possis, quam venerari ad
caedem proficisens solebas, a cujus [7]altaribus saepe istam
impiam dexteram ad necem civium transtulisti.

X.—25. Ibis tandem aliquando, quo te jam pridem ista
[1]cupiditas effrenata ac furiosa rapiebat. Neque enim tibi
haec res adfert dolorem, sed [2]quandam incredibilem
voluptatem. [3]Ad hanc te amentiam natura peperit,
voluntas exercuit, fortuna servavit. Nunquam tu [4]non
modo [5]otium, sed ne bellum quidem, nisi [6]nefarium concu-
pisti. [7]Nanctus es ex perditis atque ab omni non modo
fortuna, verum etiam spe derelictis [8]conflatam, impro-
borum manum. 26. [1]Hic tu qua laetitia perfruere! quibus
gaudiis exsultabis! quanta in voluptate bacchabere, cum
in tanto numero tuorum neque audies virum bonum
quemquam neque videbis. [2]Ad hujus vitae studium medi-
tati illi sunt, qui feruntur, labores tui, (jacere humi, non
solum [3]ad obsidendum stuprum, verum etiam [4]ad facinus
obeundum, vigilare non solum insidiantem somno mari-
torum, verum etiam bonis otiosorum) [5]Habes, ubi os-
tentes, illam tuam praeclaram patientiam famis, frigoris,
inopiae rerum omnium, [6]quibus te brevi tempore confec-
tum senties. 27. [1]Tantum profeci tum, [2]cum te a consu-
latu reppuli, ut [3]exsul potius tentare quam consul vexare

rem publicam posses atque ut id, quod est abs te scele-
rate susceptum, latrocinium potius quam bellum nomin-
aretur. ✗

XI.—Nunc ut a me, patres conscripti, quandam prope
justam patriae querimoniam ¹detester ac deprecer, per-
cipite, ⁵quaeso, diligenter quae dicam, et ea penitus animis
vestris mentibusque mandate.   Etenim si mecum patria,
quae mihi vita mea multo carior est, si cuncta Italia, si
omnis res publica sic ⁶loquatur ; ' M. Tulli, quid agis ?
⁷Tune eum, quem esse hostem comperisti, quem ducem
belli futurum vides, quem exspectari imperatorem in
castris hostium sentis, auctorem sceleris, principem
conjurationis, ⁸evocatorem servorum et civium perditorum,
exire patiere, ut abs te non ⁹emissus ex urbe, sed immisus
in urbem videatur ? Nonne ¹⁰hunc in vincula duci, non ad
mortem rapi, non summo supplicio ¹¹mactari imperabis ?
28. Quid ¹tandem te impedit ? Mosne majorum ? ²At
persaepe etiam privati in hac re publica perniciosos cives
morte multarunt. ³An leges, quae de civium Roman-
orum supplicio rogatae sunt ? At nunquam in hac urbe,
qui a re publica defecerunt, civium jura tenuerunt. An
invidiam posteritatis times ? ⁵Praeclaram vero populo
Romano refers gratiam, qui te, ⁶hominem per te cogni-
tum, nulla commendatione majorum tam mature ad sum-
mum imperium per omnes honorum gradus extulit, si
⁷propter invidiam aut alicujus periculi metum salutem
civium tuorum neglegis. | 29. Sed si quis est invidiae
metus, ¹num est vehementius severitatis ac fortitudinis
invidia quam inertiae ac nequitiae pertimescenda ? An
cum bello vastabitur Italia, vexabuntur urbes, tecta
ardebunt, tum te non existimas invidiae incendio confla-
graturum ?'

XII.—His ego sanctissimis rei publicae vocibus et
eorum hominum, qui hoc idem sentiunt, mentibus pauca

respondebo. Ego, si hoc optimum [2]f̶a̶c̶t̶u̶ [3]judicarem,
patres conscripti, Catilinam morte multari, [4]unius u̶s̶u̶r̶a̶m̶
horae [5]gladiatori isti, ad v̶i̶v̶e̶n̶d̶u̶m̶ non dedissem.
[6]Etenim si [7]summi v̶i̶r̶i̶ et clarissimi cives Saturnini et
Gracchorum et Flacci et superiorum complurium san-
guine non modo se non contaminarunt, sed etiam [8]hones-
tarunt, certe verendum mihi non erat, ne quid hoc parri-
cida civium interfecto invidiae mihi in posteritatem re-
dundaret. Quodsi ea mihi maxime impenderet, tamen
hoc animo fui semper, ut invidiam virtute partam gloriam,
non invidiam putarem. 30. [1]Quamquam nonnulli sunt in
hoc ordine, [2]qui aut ea quae imminent non videant, aut
quae vident dissimulent: [3]qui spem Catilinae mollibus
sententiis aluerunt conjurationemque nascentem non
credendo corroboraverunt ; quorum auctoritatem secuti
multi, non solum improbi, verum etiam imperiti, [4]si in
hunc animadvertissem, crudeliter et regie factum esse
dicerent. Nunc intellego, si iste, quo intendit, in Man-
liana castra [5]pervenerit, neminem tam stultum fore qui non
videat conjurationem esse factam, neminem tam impro-
bum qui non fateatur. Hoc autem uno interfecto intel-
lego hanc rei publicae pestem [6]paulisper reprimi, non in
perpetuum comprimi posse. Quodsi [7]se ejecerit secumque
suos eduxerit et eodem [8]ceteros undique collectos naufragos adgregaverit, exstinguetur atque delebitur non
modo haec [9]tam adulta rei publicae pestis, verum etiam
stirps ac semen malorum omnium.

XIII.—31. Etenim [1]jam diu, patres conscripti, in his
periculis conjurationis insidiisque versamur, sed nescio
quo pacto [2]omnium scelerum ac veteris furoris et audaciae
maturitas in nostri consulatus tempus erupit. Quodsi
[3]ex tanto latrocinio iste unus tolletur, videbimur fortasse
ad breve quoddam tempus cura et metu esse relevati,
periculum autem residebit et erit inclusum penitus in

venis atque [4]in visceribus rei publicae. Ut saepe homines
aegri morbo gravi, [5]cum aestu febrique jactantur, si aquam
gelidam [6]biberunt, primo relevari videntur, deinde multo
gravius vehementiusque adflictantur, sic hic morbus, [7]qui
est in re publica, relevatus istius poena, [8]vehementius
vivis reliquis ingravescet. 32. Quare secedant improbi,
secernant se a bonis, unum in locum congregentur, muro
denique, id quod saepe jam dixi, discernantur a nobis :
desinant insidiari domi suae consuli, circumstare tribunal
[1]praetoris urbani, [2]obsidere cum gladiis curiam, [3]malleolos
et faces ad inflammandam urbem comparare : sit denique
inscriptum in fronte unius cujusque, [4]quid de re publica
sentiat. Polliceor vobis hoc, patres conscripti, tantam
in nobis consulibus fore diligentiam, tantam in vobis
auctoritatem, tantam in equitibus Romanis virtutem,
tantam in omnibus bonis consensionem, ut Catilinae
profectione [5]omnia patefacta, inlustrata, oppressa vindicata
esse videatis. 33. [1]Hisce omnibus, Catilina, [2]cum summa
rei publicae salute, cum tua peste ac pernicie cumque
eorum exitio, qui se tecum omni scelere parricidioque
junxerunt, proficiscere ad impium bellum ac nefarium.
Tum, [3]tu, Juppiter, qui isdem quibus haec urbs [4]auspiciis
a Romulo es constitutus, quem [5]Statorem hujus urbis atque
imperii vere nominamus, hunc et hujus socios a tuis aris
ceterisque templis, a tectis urbis ac moenibus a vita for-
tunisque civium [6]arcebis, et homines bonorum inimicos,
hostes patriae, latrones Italiae, scelerum foedere inter se
ac nefaria societate conjunctos, aeternis suppliciis vivos
mortuosque mactabis.

NOTES.

CHAPTER I.

§ 1.—¹*quosque—nostra*? "How far, then, Catiline, will you trample upon our patience?" The abrupt opening of the speech shows the feelings of the orator whose indignation was naturally aroused when the conspirator dared to appear in the Senate after being declared a public enemy (*hostis patriae*).—*tandem*: "pray:" cp. δῆτα. —*abutere*: a future, as shown by *eludet*, *jactabit*. Cicero prefers the more poetic termination—*re* to—*ris* in the imperf. and fut. indic. and in the pres. and impf. subj. pass. In the pres. indic. he rarely uses it. Madvig. § 114.6.— *nostra*: Cicero includes the Senators and Consuls.

²*etiam*: "still," belongs to *quamdiu*.

³*furor iste*: note the energy imparted by personifying *furor* and *audacia.*—*iste* is strictly a pronoun demonstrative of the second person: *iste locus*, "the place where you are standing:" *ista verba*: "the words you utter." It often had a contemptuous meaning in Cicero's orations.

⁴*eludet*: "will turn us into mockery:" a gladiatorial term of avoiding a thrust by the rapid movement of the body: hence, to baffle,. deceive, and, as here, to mock. *Nos* is omitted by some editors.

⁵*quem—audacia*: "to what length will your unbridled audacity proceed?"—*quem ad finem* = *quousque* or *quamdiu*. According to Schultz *quousque* puts the more general question of *time* and *degree*: *quamdiu*, the more special question, of *time* only: *quem ad finem*: of *degree* only.

⁶*jactabit* = *insolenter se efferet*: *se jactare*, "to toss the head contemptuously," "to walk with a conceited swing."

⁷*nihilne—moverunt*? "Have the guards nightly stationed on the Palatine nothing daunted you? Nothing, the sentinels of the city; nothing, the trepidation of the people; nothing, the throng together of all patriotic (citizens); nothing, this most impregnable place for convening the Senate; nothing, the countenances and looks of these?" Observe the emphatic position of *nihil* in the beginning of successive clauses (*anaphora*).— *Palatii*: the Palatine hill was adjacent to the Forum. It was

here that Augustus built a splendid mansion : hence our word
palace from the residence of the emperor built on the *Palatium*.
In times of danger the Palatium, one of the most important
military posts of the city, was occupied by a guard. Originally
the word meant the "feeding place :" root *pal, pascere:* cp.
Pales, Palilia. Varro derives it from *pal,* "to wander :" cp.
palor. It may have been the "common" for cattle in early
days. *Vigiliae :* under the republic, on emergencies, the *trium-
viri capitales, aediles* or *tribuni plebis* acting as a kind of police appointed night watches to keep order.—*timor populi :* cp. Sallust.
Cat.: C. 31 : *immutata urbis facies erat : ex summa laetitia atque
lascivia . . . repente omnes tristitia invasit.*—*bonorum cmnium :*
with *bonus :* cp. ἀγαθός, often used in the sense of "patriotic,"
opposed to *malus civis,* κακός : "unpatriotic."—*locus :* the
Senate was usually convened on the Kalends, Nones and Ides of
each month, and the meeting usually held in the Curia Hostilia.
Extraordinary meetings (*senatus indictus*) as the present one
were convened in some temple, or other place consecrated by
the augurs. The present meeting was held in the temple of
Juppiter Stator, near the *via sacra,* at the foot of the Palatine,
which might be said to be *munitissimus* from the special guard
there as well as from its position.—*ora vultusque :* the former
denotes the natural and habitual state, as expressed by the
mouth and the lower part of the face : while the latter indicates
the temporary and changing state, as expressed by the motion
of the eye and brow.

[8]*constrictam—vides :* "do you not see that your conspiracy
has already come within the privity of all these ?" literally, "is
held bound by." Orelli distinguishes between *non* and *nonne*
in direct questions. Where *non* is used, the speaker, sure
of his opinion, does not heed the answer of the opponent :
where *nonne* is used, the speaker expects and wishes that the
person questioned will agree with him.—*constrictam teneri :* the
metaphor is taken from chaining a wild beast to which he here
compares the conspiracy.

[9]*proxima :* this speech was delivered November 8th : so *nox
proxima* would be the night of 7th : *nox superior,* the night of
the 6th, also called *nox prior,* § 8. On this occasion they were
at the house of M. Porcius Laeca. What they did on the *nox
proxima* we are not informed.—*egeris, fueris, convocaveris,
ceperis :* subjunctive of dependent question : H. 529, I.

[10]*nostrûm :* distinguish *nostrum* uses partitively and *nostri*
used possessively.

§ 2.—[1]*vivit ? immo vero :* Cicero often connects a word by
putting that word in the form of a question with or without

dicam and answering it by *immo*. According to Madvig. (§ 454) *immo* corrects a former statement as being quite inaccurate, or too weak, though true as far as it goes.—*immo vero:* "nay, indeed."

[2]*in senatum venit:* as *vir praetorius* Catiline had a right to enter the Senate.

[3]*notat et designat:* a metaphor from the marking of the animals appointed for sacrifice. Cicero often uses synonymous words to impress the idea more strongly.: "he marks and stamps each one of us for slaughter :" cp. Leg. Man. 3, 7. *Cives Romanos necandos trucidandosque denotavit.*

[4]*viri fortes :* ironical.

[5]*videmur*, scil. *nobis:* "we fancy that we are doing our duty to the state."

[6]*si —vitemus :* for the subj. in *protasis*, and indic. in *apodosis*, see H. 511.

[7]*ad mortem—opportebat :* "to death long ago, O Catiline, ought you to have been dragged by the order of the consul ?" Note the emphatic position of *ad mortem.*—*duci:* for the present inf : see. H., 537, I.—*jussu consulis:* the Senate had entrusted the safety of the State by the *decretum ultimum* (*videant consules, ne quid detrimenti respublica capiat*). By the power vested in the consuls in consequence of this decree they had the power to put Catiline to death.

[8]*in te—machinaris :* "On you should that ruin long since have been hurled which you for a long time have been plotting against us all." Join *jampridem* from the previous clause with *conferri*. The present tense in Latin with *jamdiu* includes past tense : cf. πάλαι λέγω, *jamdiu dico :* "I have long ago told you and do so still."—*machinari* ; μηχανᾶσθαι, to plan by *artful* and *secret* means : *moliri*, to plan by *strong* effort.

§ 3. [1]*An vero :* the original force of *an* is "or," and when used interrogatively the sentence is elliptical. Here we may supply: "Am I right in my conjecture, or, in fact, did that illustrious man, P. Scipio, chief pontiff, though filling no magistracy, slay Tiberius Gracchus when slightly disturbing the settled order of the State." We may conveniently translate here *an vero* by : "while, in fact." The argument here is *a minore ad majus*. P. Cornelius Scipio Nasica consul with D. Junius Brutus 138 B.C. Cicero probably adds *pontifex maximus* to remind his hearers of the high dignity and prudence which a man gifted with this office would possess. He also uses *privatus* because in contrast to *consules*, the office of *pontifex maximus* not being a *magistratus. Tiberium Grac-*

chum: see Proper Names—*mediocriter labefactantem*: Cicero designedly extenuates the guilt of Gracchus to heighten the crimes of Catiline. In fact, the orator represents the guilt of Gracchus in different lights according to the exigencies of his cause: cp. De Leg. Ag., 2, 5, 10: De Off. II., 12. 43. *Catilinam*: emphatic position: "Catiline, desiring to devastate the world with sword and fire shall we consuls tolerate?"— *orbis terrae*: there is little difference between *orbis terrae* and *orbis terrarum*.—*caede atque incendiis*: also *ferro et igni*.

²*illa*: "the following instance:" though only the case of Ahala is mentioned, the plural is probably used to intimate that other cases might be adduced.

³*C. Servilius Ahala*: see Proper Names.

⁴*novis—studentem*: "aiming to overturn the government:" cp. νεωτερίζειν.

⁶*fuit-fuit*: note the emphatic repetition of the word (*epizeuxis*). *ista virtus*: here *ista=illa*: "that well-known public spirit:" We may take *virtus=amor patriae*: "patriotism."

⁶*ut—coercerent*: "that brave men inflicted severer punishment on a factious citizen then on the bitterest foe"—*suppliciis*: abl. means.

⁷*senatus consultum*: the decree arming the consuls with civil and military power. The formula was *videant consules ne quid respublica detrimenti capiat*.

⁸*vehemens et grave*: "full of force and severity."

⁹*rei publicae*: generally taken as a dative after *deest*: others take it as a genitive depending on *consilium*, i.e., there is no lack of precedents of the state, i.e., the state have many instances of wicked citizens being punished. The state, according to Cicero, has enough of wisdom (*consilium*) and determining authority (*auctoritas*), but the executive power is weak.

CHAPTER II.

§ 4. ¹*quondam*: B.C. 121: see *C. Gracchus*, in Proper Names. In a decree of this kind both consuls were named. The other, Q. Fabius, was at that time in that part of Gaul known afterwards as Provincia, and his absence from Rome may account for the omission of his name from the decree.

²*intercessit*: i.e., between the passing of the decree and the death of Gracchus.

³*propter—suspiciones*: another case of extenuation to bring out more vividly the guilt of Catiline. Distinguish *suspicio, suspicio*.

3

⁵*patre-majoribus*, scil, *ortus*: abl. of origin. The father of C. Sempronius Gracchus was Tib. Sempronius Gracchus, who twice held the consulship (B.C. 177, and B.C. 163), the censorship (169 B.C.), twice enjoyed a triumph, once over the Celtiberians, 178 B.C., and once over the Sardinians, 175 B.C. The mother of the Gracchi was Cornelia, daughter of P. Scipio Africanus Major, who defeated Hannibal at Zama B.C. 202. Thus Gracchus united in himself two of the noblest families in Rome.

⁵*M. Fulvius*: one of the commissioners appointed to carry out the *lex agraria* of C. Gracchus. He was killed with his eldest son in the fray in which Gracchus was slain. The youngest son was killed after the conflict.

⁶*simili-publica*: some omit the commas after *senatusconsulto* and *consulibus* and thus make *Mario*, *Valerio* datives ; others retain the commas and make these words ablative absolute. The event happened in the sixth consulship of Marius, B.C. 102. Lucius Saturninus and C. Servilius Glaucia were guilty of killing C. Memmius who was seeking the consulship. Both Saturninus and Glaucia were driven into the Capitol and put to death.

⁷*num—est*? "Did the punishment of death inflicted by the state cause L. Saturninus, the tribune of the people, and C. Servilius, the praetor, to wait for a single day?"—*mors ac rei publicae poena = mortis poena a re publica inflicta*. *at vero*: "but we assuredly."

⁸*vicesimum diem*: the 18th day since the *senatus consultum* was passed. The decree was passed Oct. 21st and this oration was delivered Nov. 8th. The Romans, however, reckoned both days.

⁹*aciei*: "the edge:" root *ac*: "sharp."

¹⁰*inclusum in tabulis*: "shut up among our records" i.e. a useless decree unless carried into effect.

¹¹*quo—convenit*: "and in accordance with this decree, you, O Catiline, should be at once put to death:" with *confestim*: cp. *festino*.

¹²*et vivis*: rhetorical for *et vivis quidem* or *idque.—cupio—cupio*: "I desire, on the one hand,—I am anxious, on the other."—The acc. of pronouns gives more prominence to the circumstance wished by disconnecting it from the *cupio*.

¹³*dissolutus*: "remiss," "forgetful of duty." Synonymous with *neglegens*.

¹⁴*inertiae nequitiaeque*: "of sloth and irresolution."

§ 5.—¹*castra—collocata* : "a camp is pitched," at Faesulae (now *Fiesole*), which lies on a spur of the western slope of the Appenines, not far from Florence. At this place Manlius had collected a number of soldiers who had served under Sulla. § 7. The term *fauces*, literally "jaws," is often used for a mountain pass : cp. Scott : Lady of the Lake : "Led slowly through the pass's jaws."

²*in dies singulos* : "daily," always joined to some word of comparative force and expressing daily increase or diminution : *cottidie*, simply daily repetition.—*imperatorem ducemque* : *impe-rator*, a military leader deriving his authority from the Senate : *dux*, simply a leader.

³*adeo in Senatu* : "in the very Senate," or as Zumpt (§ 737) takes it, "nay more," "nay even in the Senate."—*jam* : "now at once."—*jussero* : the fut. pf. often represents the speedy ac-complishment of a fut. action.

⁵*credo* : used ironically : cp. οἶομαι. Here the word may be equivalent to *non erit verendum*.

⁶*verendum mihi*, etc.: "I shall have to fear (i.e. I am con-vinced) that all patriots will regard your death as occuring too late, rather than as too severe and cruel," or as Wilkin's translates : "Certainly it is more likely that all patriots will consider this action too late, than that anyone should consider it too cruel." Explain *quisquam.*

⁷*certe—adducor* : "for a certain reason, I am not yet led to do :" i.e. the fear of punishing Catiline before his guilt was fully ascertained lest he might pass for an injured man with his sympathizers. Cicero's object was to cause Catiline and his associates to leave Rome.

⁸*interficiere* : i.e. "you will ordered to be put to death." Others read *interficiam te.*

⁹*tui similis* : *similis* in Cicero generally takes *genitive or dative* of persons : *dative* of things.

¹⁰*qui = ut is* : "as not to confess that it was justly inflicted:"— *id*, i.e. *te interficiam* from *interficiere* before.

§ 6.—¹*quisquam* : for use, see H. 457.

²*multis—oppressus* : "beset by many powerful guards placed by me :" note the idiom. Cicero had guards placed not only in the capital, but also throughout Italy.

³*te commovere*: "to make any farther movement :" a meta-phor taken from the gladiatorial contests.

⁴*fecerunt = speculati sunt et custodiverunt* : the verb *facio* in Latin, and ποιώ in Greek, and *do* in English, are often used as substitutes for other verbs.

CHAPTER III.

[5]*Etenim—potest?* This gives a reason for the clause *sed vives—possis.*

[6]*exspectes* : H. 503, I.

[7]*coeptus nefarios* . "your traitorous attempts:" another reading is *coetus.*

[8]*privata domus* : the house of M. Porcius Laeca.

[9]*parietibus* : abl. means. Distinguish *moenia* (root *mun*, to defend : cp. ἀμύνειν, the walls of a city for defensive purposes : *murus* (= *mun-rus*), any kind of wall : *paries* (root *par*, to separate) : the partition walls of a house : *maceria*, a garden wall.

[10]*voces conjurationis = voces conjuratorum* : "the voices of the conspirators :" Cicero often uses abstract for concrete terms.

[11]*inlustrantur* opposed to *obscurare* as *crumpunt* to *domus . . continet.*

[12]*istam mentem* : "that resolve of thine," i.e. of remaining in the city to murder the people.

[13]*mihi crede = me sequere* : "follow my advice :" *mihi crede* is the common order in Cicero : *crede mihi* in other writers.

[14]*teneris undique* : "you are hemmed in (i.e. convicted) on every hand."

[15]*quae—recognoscas* : "and these plans you may now review with me :" Construe : *quae* (= *et haec*, scil. *consilia*) *licet* (*tibi ut*) *recognoscas jam mecum.*

§ 7.—[1]*meministine = nonne meministi* : the particle *-ne* added to a verb has sometimes in Cicero the force of *nonne.* Cp. Cat. Major, C. 10, *videtisne = nonne videtis.* So frequently in Terence, Plautus, and in colloquial Latin : H. 396, II. 1.

[2]*ante-Novembres* : "on the 12th day before the Kalends of November," i.e. on October 21st. This anomolous mode of expression probably arose from the transposition of *ante.* Having one written *ante die duodecimo Kalendas*, they would easily be led to infer that *ante* governed *die* and so would write *ante diem duodecimum Kalendas.* For the method of computation of time among the Romans, see H. 642.

[3]*certo die, qui dies* : the repetition of the subst. after the relation may be explained on the ground of clearness.

[4]*audaciae—tuae :* "the partisan and agent of your audacious schemes." The words *satelles* and *administer* are synonymous,

the former being more poetical and explained by the latter, which is the more common.

[6]*num—ilies ?* "was I, O Catiline, ignorant not merely of an attempt so enormous, so wicked, so surpassing belief, but, a thing which is more to be wondered at, of the day ?"—*me fallit :* cf. *latet me, λανθάνει με.*

[6]*caedem—Novembres :* "that you had fixed the 28th October for the slaughter of the nobles." The construction is *in diem quintum ante Kalendas Novembres.* Predetermination of future time is often expressed by *in* with acc.: as *in diem posterum senatum convocavit,* not " he summoned the Senate *on* the next day," but "*for* the next day."

[7]*optimatium :* is the only word, not a proper name, in—*at,* that makes the gen. pl. in—*ium. Roma :* Give rules for the construction of the names of towns.

[8]*sui conservandi :* sui like *nostri, vestri* is not a gen. pl. but a gen. sing. of an adj. used collectively and abstractly : "not for self-preservation :" Madvig, 297, b. c. : 417.

[9]*reprimendorum :* here used in the sense of *impediendorum :*" " of preventing your plans being carried out." This is probably a rhetorical flourish on the part of Cicero, as no such fact is mentioned by Sallust. Among those who fled, according to Plutarch, was M. Crassus. *num—dicebas !* "Can you deny that on that very day, beset by the guards I had placed, by my watchfulness, you could take not one step against the state, when on the departure of the others you, nevertheless, expressed your-self satisfied with the murder of us who remained ? "—*discessu ceterorum :* the ablative here supplies the place of a participial abl. absol. —*nostra—caede—qui :* the relative is made to refer to an antecedent implied in *nostra :* H. 445, 6,—*quum :* is often used by Cicero in the impf. indic. when the bare notion of time or of continuance is to be expressed.—*remansissemus :* virtual oblique narrative : hence the subjunctive.

§ 8. — [1]*quid :* "further" : lit. "what shall I say ?" scil. *dicam.*

[2]*te—occupaturum :* "that you would anticipate us in seizing Praeneste in an attack by night on the first of November." With *occupare :* cp. φθάνειν : no other writer mentions this fact. —*ipsis : ipse* denotes exactness in temporal expressions : *triginta ipsi dies,* " exactly thirty days."

[3]*sensistisne = nonne sensistis :* see note 1, § 7, above.

[4]*praesidium,* a guard in a general sense : *custodiae,* watches on the wall : *vigiliae,* night watches.

⁵nihil—nihil, nihil: see note 7, § 1. "There is nothing you do, nothing you plan, nothing you think which I do not hear only, but also see or clearly perceive." Some read *non modo* for *non modo non*, which the senses requires.

CHAPTER IV.

⁶tandem: see note 1, § 1. The orator implies by this particle the fulness of his knowledge.

noctem illam superiorem: "the events on the night preceding the last:" i.e., the events on the night of the 6th November, when the meeting was held at the house of M. Porcius Laeca. —*illam* here does duty for the definite article in English.

⁸jam—reipublicae: "You shall presently perceive that I am much more actively watchful for the safety of the state than you are for its destruction"—*intelliges*: what compounds of—*lego* have *lexi* in the perfect?—*acrius*?

⁹dico: this passage is executed with fine skill. At first the orator states the fact clearly and briefly. He notes the effect on the conspirator and calls for an answer: after no reply is given, Cicero goes into details.

¹⁰priore nocte: "on the night preceding (the last)": a change for *superiore nocte*. Others say it means *initio noctis*.

¹¹inter falcarios, scil, *opifices*: "through the scythe makers' street:" a street in Rome deriving its name from the occupation of its inhabitants. Cp. Isocr. Areopag. § 48: ἐν ταῖς αὐλητρίσιν: Livy, 35, 43: *inter lignarios* "in the woodcutters' street."

¹²in—domum: is the preposition necessary?

¹⁸complures: Sallust (Cat. 17) gives the names of eleven senators who were present on this occasion.

¹⁴amentiae: distinguish *amentia* and *dementia*.

¹⁶convincam: "I will prove it."

§ 9. *¹ubinam gentium sumus*! This phrase is very much the same as ours, "where in the world are we?" It is often used in rhetorical writings and in the comic poets. For the partitive genitive, see H. 397, 4.

²hic, hic: Epizeuxis: note the emphatic repetition.

³patres conscripti: said to be for *patres et conscripti*. The senators were called *patres*. In the wars of the early republic many were killed. To fill the place of those slain some were summoned (*conscripti*.) Hence the original senators—those summoned—were addressed as *patres et conscripti*: afterwards the *et* was omitted.

[4]*in—consilio* : " in this most venerable and respectable assembly of the whole world." The term *sanctus* applied to the senate may refer to the building in which it was convened. The usual distinction between *consilium* and *concilium*, that the former means advice, plans, while the latter means an assemblage, with regard to those who compose it, does not hold good. The roots of these words are different, *consilium* : from *con, sed*, to sit : cp. *sedes, solium, ἑδος* ; for the change of *d* to *l* : cp. *δάκρυ*, lacrima ; *olere, odere.—concilium : con, cai*, to summon : cp. *Kalendae, calare, καλεῖν*.

[5]*qui—cogitent* : " (are men so nefarious) as to plan the destruc- tion of every one of us, and the ruin of this city and further of the whole world."—*qui = tales ut.—adeo* : literally, " up to this point :" then, " in fact."

[6]*sententiam rogo* : supply *hos* from the preceding. *Sententiam vogo* is said of the presiding magistrate who, in proposing a *senatus consultum*, asked individually the will of the senators.

[7]*vulnero* : by mentioning their names publicly.

[8]*igitur* : resumes (*analeptic*) the argument referring to the question, *num rogare audes ?* Catiline had left this unanswered. Having been interrupted by the outbreak of his indignation, the orator now returns to the doings of the conspirators at the house of Laeca.

[9]*distribuisti* : Sallust (C. 27) informs us that C. Manlius was sent to Faesulae, and the adjoining territory of Etruria : Septimius, into the Picene territory : C. Julius, into Apulia.

[10]*statuisti—placeret* : scil : *locum* : " you appointed the place to which it was agreed on that each should set out :" For sub- junctive in *placeret*, see H. 529, I.

[11]*delegisti—educeres* : " you picked out those whom you were to leave at Rome, whom you were to take with you." Sallust (Cat. C. 43) says that Statilius and Gabinius were to set fire to the city, and Cethegus was to assassinate Cicero, and Lentulus to superintend the general massacre.

[12]*discripsisti* : *discribo* is used where the fundamental notion is to map out, plan, arrange, put in order, as *distribuere, dividere, disponere* : *describo* is to write down, to compose. Sallust (Cat. C. 43) says that the conspirators were to fire twelve (Plutarch says a hundred) parts of the city at one and the same time. For *discripsisti* : cf. Cic. Pro Sulla, 8 : *Tam Catilina dies exurendi tum caeteris manendi conditio, tum discriptio totam per orbem caedis atque incendiorum constituta est.*

[13]*paullulum—morae* : " that you still had even now a slight cause of delay." *Paullulus* is a dual diminutive for *paurululus* =

paullulus : *u* being omitted before the first *l* and the *r* assimilated : cp. *sterula* = *stella.—viverem* : subj.: giving the opinion of Catiline.

[14]*etiam tum* : is used to express the words of Catilina, not those of Cicero.

[14]*duo equites* : according to Cic. (Pro Sulla, 18, 52) one was C. Cornelius : Sallust (Cat. C. 18) mentions the Senator L. Vargunteius as the other.

[16]*qui—liberarent* : "to free you from the fear you had :" *qui =* *tales ut.*

illa ipsa nocte : these knights were to pay their intended visit in the morning, where the Roman magistrates and distinguished men held their audiences and received their clients.

[17]*lectulo* : the diminutive here has scarcely any force. There may be a slight reference to its comfort : "my dear bed."

§ 10.—[1]*vixdum—dimisso* : "when your meeting was hardly as yet broken up."

Comperi : Cicero gained his knowledge from Curius and Fulvia (Sall. Cat. C. 28). According to Merivale, Cicero used *comperio* when he was wont to indicate his knowledge of facts, though afraid of revealing the sources of his information. The word does not always have this force.

[2]*salutatum* : supine after a verb of motion. What different ways of expressing a purpose in Latin ?

[8]*mane*: another form is *mani*: cp. *luci, heri*, locatives.

[4]*id temporis* : for partitive genitive : H. 397, note 5.

CHAPTER V.

§ 11.—[1]*quae—sint* : "since these facts are so :" often used to sum up a chain of facts founded on evidence.

[2]*perge quo coepisti*, scil. *pergere* : "proceed as you have begun." Conjugate *pergere*.

desiderant : "feel the loss of."—*desiderare*, to feel the loss of an object of love or sympathy : hence "to yearn after;" *requirere* : to feel the loss of a thing, as an act of the understanding.

[8]*si minus* = *si non.* Construe : *si minus (educis omnes, educ) quam plurimos (educere potes)*.

[4]*dummodo—intersit* : cp. Plutarch (Cicero 16) : "and Cicero arising ordered him to leave the city ; for while he himself

carried on his political contest by words and Catiline by arms, there must needs be a city wall between them."

5non—sinam : note the *anaphora.* Cicero uses three synonymous verbs to express the thought that he will not endure the conduct of Catiline under any circumstances. We may translate : " I cannot, will not, shall not endure it."

6magna—urbis : " much gratitude is due to the immortal gods and especially (*atque*) to this Juppiter Stator, the most ancient guardian of our city." Distinguish *gratiam habere,* to feel thankful : *gratias agere,* to return thanks in words : *gratiam referre,* to show oneself thankful by deeds. Juppiter obtained the name Stator because he is said to have stayed the flight of the Romans when they were hard pressed by the Sabines. The place where the flight was arrested was marked by a temple vowed by Romulus at the foot of the Palatine (Livy I. 12).

7quod—effugimus : " because we have already escaped so often a pest so cruel, so dreadful, so dangerous to the state "—*toties* : referring to the earlier conspiracy of Catiline which failed.

8non—reipublicae : " it must not again and again depend on one man that the existence of the state should be in peril :" or, " the safety of the state must not be often exposed to danger by one man." A similar expression is found : Cic. Pro. Rosc. Amer. 51.148 : *summa res publica in hujus periculo tentatur.*

9consuli designato : in the days of Cicero the consuls were elected on the 22nd October, but did not formally enter upon their office till January 1st. Between the time of their election and entering upon office they were called *consules designati. proximis comitiis consularibus* : referring to Oct. 22nd.

10in campo, scil. *Martio* : the consular elections were held in the Campus Martius, a plain between the city and the Tiber.

11competitores : D. Junius Silanus and L. Licinius Murena.

12compressi—copiis : on the day of the consular elections, we are told by Plutarch, Cicero put on a coat of mail and was attended by the chief men of Rome and a great number of youths to the Campus Martius. He there threw off his *toga* and displayed his coat of mail to show the danger to which he was exposed. The people were so angry with Catiline that they chose Murena and Silanus as consuls.

13quotiescumque—obstiti : " as often as you aimed at my life, by my own resources did I oppose you :" *petere* is a gladiatorial term, " to aim a blow at an opponent."

14quamquam videbam : distinguish *quamquam,* introducing a conceded fact and in good authors used with the indicative from *quamvis* introducing a purely hypothetical case and used with the subjunctive. H., 516, I. and II.

[15]*perniciem—conjunctum* : "that my destruction was linked with the signal downfall of the state"—*pernicies* : from *per*- root *nec* : cp. *nex, noceo,* hence utter destruction—*calamitas* : another form is *cadamitas* : from *cado,* to fall : for the interchange of *d* and *l* : cp. *odere, olere* : *dingua, lingua.*

§ 12. [1]*nunc jam* : emphatically, "now"—*jam nunc* : is "even now" (i.e., before the regular time), or "now at last."

[2]*denique* : "in a word."

[3]*quare—audeo* : "wherefore since I do not yet dare to pursue that course which first presents itself and which is in accordance with the power (I hold) and the principles of our ancestors"—*imperii* genitive after *proprium.* What cases may *proprius* govern ?—*imperii* refers to the extraordinary power which he had by the decree *videant consules ne quid detrimenti respublica capiat.* This decree (*decretum ultimum*) armed the consuls with civil and military an ty. Others say *imperii proprium* means, "in accordance with this government."

[4]*ad—lenius* : "milder as regards severity," or "in point of severity." *Ad = quoad, quoad attinet ad, si spectes.* He uses *ad communem salutem utilius* to balance *ad severitatem lenius.*

[5]*reliqua—manus* : "a remnant of the conspirators." Ernesti reads *aliqua* for *reliqua.*

[6]*sin* : "if, on the other hand."

[7]*exhaurietur—reipublicae* : "there shall be drained off from the city a great and destructive refuse of the state composed of your comrades." *Exhaurio* : cp. ἀντλέω properly to drain the bilge water (ἀντλος *sentina*) out of the hold of a vessel.—*tuorum comitum* : this secondary genitive is one of explanation (*expexegetical*).

§ 13. [1]*imperante me* : abl. absolute.

[2]*faciebas = facere volebas* : Madvig, § 337, obs. I.

[3]*consul hostem* : note the emphatic juxtaposition of these words.

[4]*num—exilium,* scil, *jubes me exire* : "You do not order me to go into exile, do you ?" Distinguish *exilium, deportatio,* and *relegatio* : see Antiquities.

[5]*me consulis* : distinguish *me consulit, mihi consulit, in me consulit.*

CHAPTER VI.

[6]*quod—possit*: H., 503, I.

[7]*extra—hominum*: "unconnected with that band of conspira‑tors composed of worthless men"—*conjuratio*: used in a con‑crete sense: cp. *advocatio, servitium*. For subjunctive: H., 500, I.

[8]*quae—est?* "what stain of domestic infamy has not been branded on your life?" Distinguish: *nŏtă, nōtă, nŏtă.* The expression *nota domesticae turpitudinis* differs in meaning from *privatarum rerum dedecus*: the former relates to moral or immoral domestic life, the latter to all private actions as op‑posed to those that affect a man's public character. *Nota* is applied (1) to the brand on cattle; Virg. Georg. 3, 158: (2) to the mark placed on a fugitive slave when retaken: (3) to the mark placed by the censor (*nota censoria*) on revising the list of citizens, opposite the name of the person degraded. Accord‑ing to Plutarch, Catiline had slain his own brother and murdered his own son that there might be no obstacle to his marrying Aurelia Orestilla.

[9]*quod—fama*: "what scandal in private life does not cling to your notorious acts?" Some read *infamiae*, a dat, after *haeret*, which is sometimes found. Give the different construc‑tions of *haerere*.

[10]*quae—afuit*: "what act of impurity ever was strange to your eyes, what enormity to your hands, what pollution to your whole body?"—*libido*; licentiousness, in a general sense ; *facinus*, a bold, daring deed, in a bad sense, unless justified by some favourable epithet : *flagitium*, a disgraceful, lustful excess.

[11]*cui—praetulisti?* "to what youth, after you had once en‑tangled him by the allurements of vice, did you not hand either a dagger to commit some daring deed, or a torch to inflame his passion?" *adulescentulo* : the diminutive is used in a depre‑ciatory sense, since many a weak youth was misled by Catiline (Sallust Cat., c. 14). *facem* : the figure refers to the nightly revels and debauches of Catiline. Slaves carried torches before their masters at night to show the way. The torch of Catiline not merely showed the way to crimes, but served to inflame the passions of lust.

§ 14.—[1]*quid vero?* scil, *dicam* ; "further : " lit. "what, indeed, shall I say?"

[2]*nuper—cumulasti?* " When lately by the death of your first wife you had rendered your home empty to contract a new marriage, did you not aggravate this crime by committing

another incredible act of guilt ? " It is said that Catiline poisoned his first wife and murdered his own son, to marry Aurelia Orestilla.

³*patior* : " I suffer myself : " a kind of middle form : cp. *glorior, vescor, vertor, lavor.—tanti—immanitas* : " so enormous a crime."

⁵ *quas—senties* : " which you will find wholly threaten you on the next Ides." On the *ides* it was usual to pay interest on borrowed money, cp. Hor. Ep. 2. The *ides* (*idus*, from *iduare*, to divide) were on the 13th of each month, except in March, May, July, October, when they fell on the 15th. As this oration was delivered on the 8th, Catiline had only five days to prepare against bankruptcy. Decline *idus* ? What words are fem. of 4th decl. ?

⁶*ad—pertinent* : " to these I come, which concern not the personal disgrace which attaches to your vices, (which concern) not the embarassment and scandal of your home, but (which concern) the welfare of the state and the life and safety of us all." —*ignominiam* : referring to his personal crimes.—*difficultatem* : his financial difficulties.

§ 15. ¹*cum scius* : for subjunctive : H. 522, II. 2.

²*neminem* : decline this word.

³*pridie—Januarias* : scil *ante* : " on the day before the Kalends of January," i.e. December 31st, Sallust gives an account of this earlier conspiracy. The plan was to murder the consuls in the capitol, then Catiline and Autronius were to seize the consular power. Suetonius says that both Crassus and Cæsar were partners in guilt, and that the scheme failed because Crassus did not appear at the proper time. A second time (5th February) an attempt was made, but this also failed in consequence of Catiline having given the signal too soon before a sufficient number of followers had arrived.

⁴*Lepido et Tullo consulibus* : M. Æmilius Lepidus and L. Volcatius Tullus were consuls 66 B.C. The *consules designati* were P. Autronius Paetus and P. Cornelius Sulla : but these were disqualified for bribery and L. Aurelius Cotta and L. Manlius Torquatius (their accusers) obtained the consulship.

⁵*comitio* : distinguish *comitium* and *comitia*. Where was the *comitium* ? *manum—paravisse* ? scil, *potestne——scias* : " that you collected a gang to slay the consuls and leading men of the state ?"

⁶*sceleri—obstitisse* ? " that no reflection or fear of yours, but the good luck of the state thwarted your wicked and frenzied attempt ! " Is *aliquis* commonly used in negative clauses ?

⁷*neque—postea* : i.e., *nam quae post a te commissa sunt, ea neque obscura sunt, neque pauca.*

⁸*Consulem designatum* : see note 9, § 11.

⁹*petitiones* : see note 7, § 11.

¹*ita—effugi* : "aimed in such a way that they seemed impossible to be parried have I avoided by a slight side movement, and, as they term it, by (a deflection of) the body."—*petitio, declinatio, corpus, effugio,* are terms of the fencing school purposely used by Cicero to show that Catiline was no better than a gladiator : cp. Cic. Cat. II. 2.—*ut aiunt* : cp. ὡς φασί : "as the saying is."

§ 16.—¹*tibi* : ethical dative : H. 389.—*jam* : "ere now."—*de manibus* is explanatory (*epexegetical*) to *tibi.*

²*excidit* : distinguish *excĭdit, excĭdit.*

³*quae—defigere* : the position of the relative and the indirect interrogation is foreign to our idiom, and must be avoided in translation : *quae = et haec,* scil, *sica* : "and I know not by what (unhallowed) rites it has been consecrated and devoted to its purpose by you that you deem it necessary to plunge it in the body of the consul." Cicero here refers to the fact that a human sacrifice took place at the house of Catiline, and that the dagger used on that occasion was dedicated to the purpose of slaying the consuls : cp. Sallust, Cat. C. 23.

CHAPTER VII.

⁴*tua—ista vita* : "that life that you lead."

⁵*sed ut* : construe *sed (tecum loquar) ut misericordia (permotus esse videar).*

⁶*nulla* : stronger than *non* : "not at all," "not a particle."

⁷*paullo ante* : "a moment ago."

⁸*frequentia* : "throng," : cp. *frequens senatus* : "a crowded senate," : *necessarii* : cp. ἀναγκαῖοι. — *salutavit* : among the Romans it was customary when they saw their friends or eminent men approaching to rise up, and salute or courteously address them.

⁹*post—memoriam* : "within the memory of men" : cp. Thucy. I. 7 : ἀφ' οὖ Ἕλληνες μέμνηνται.

contigit : generally means, "it befalls" of fortunate occurences, but not always.

¹⁰*vocis—contumeliam . . . judicio taciturnitatis* : Chiasmus.— *vocis—taciturnitatis = loquentium—tacitorum* : "are you waiting for reproofs from those speaking, when you are overpowered

by the most solemn sentence of those, though they are silent."
The reference is to the fact that the Senate had declared Catiline
patriae hostis, and had received him with silence on entering
the Senate.

[11]*quid?* scil. *dicam.* We often find *quid? quod* used by
Cicero in rapid rhetorical questions : Madvig., 479, d. obs. 1.

[12]*adventu tuo* : see note 9, § 7 : *abl. time.*

[13]*ista subsellia* : "the benches near you." The seats of the
senators *(subsellia)* were beneath that of the consul *(sella
curulis)*, which was on a platform.

[14]*qui fuerunt* : "who have been often destined for slaughter
by you."—*tibi* : dat. for abl. with *abs = abs te.* Distinguish
constituti sunt and *constituti fuerunt.*

[15]*nudam atque inanem :* "completely bare :" Cicero often
uses two epithets of nearly the same meaning to emphasize the
idea to be conveyed.

[16]*tandem* : see note 1, § 1.

§ 17.—[1]*servi—arbitraris* : a fine example of the argument
a fortiori. The Latins call this *amplificatio* (Quint. 8, 4, 9),
the Greeks ἐνθύμημα, a rhetorical conclusion, drawn from
opposites.

[2]*me hercule* : either (1) *me Hercules juvet*, or (2) *me, Hercules,
juves.* We also find *me hercules, mehercle, mercule,* varieties
of the same oath. For the tendency to drop *s* final : cp. Peile
(Greek and Latin Etymology, p. 355).

[3]*isto pacto* : "in the way."—*isto* here does duty for the article
or may be = *eodem.*

omnes : the fellow-conspirators are no longer regarded as
citizens by Cicero.

[4]*urbem* : scil., *relinquendam.*

[5]*injuria* : "without any just cause."

[6]*offensum = invisum, odiosum.*

[7]*infestis* : another form is *infensis* : "menacing."

[8]*agnoscas* : distinguish *agnosco, ignosco, cognosco, recognosco,*
in meaning.

[9]*dubitas—vitare :* when *dubito* means "to doubt :" *non dubito*
is properly construed with *quin* and the subjunctive, rarely with
the infinitive. But when *dubito* means "to scruple," "to
hesitate," and the sentence following contained the same subject, *non dubito* is generally construed with the infinitive.

[10]*mentes sensusque* : "souls and senses."

¹¹*aliquo* : " to some place or other."

¹²*nunc* = νῦν δέ, " but now, as it is," used to contrast *actual* and *imagined* condition.

¹³*jamdiu—cogitare* : " and for a long time has it come to the conclusion that you have been planning nothing but her ruin."—*nihil* = *de nulla re.—parricidio* = *interitu,* because *patria* is regarded *communis parens.* According to Roman law *parri-cidium* included the murder of intimate friends as well as of parents.

¹⁴*verebere : vereor,* a religious reverence due to a superior : *pertimesco,* an excessive dread of impending calamity.

§ 18.—¹*quae—loquitur :* a fine personification. Note the oxymoron in *tacita—loquitur.*

²*nullum* : note the emphatic positions of *nullum—nullum.*

³*neces* : alluding to the murders which Catiline perpetrated as a partisan of Sulla, during the dictatorship of the latter. ·

⁴*sociorum* . in 67 B.C. Catiline was propraetor of Africa. In 65 B.C. he was accused by P. Clodius Pulcher, the inveterate enemy of Cicero, for cruel oppression of the provincials, but he succeeded in buying off the accuser, and the persecution came to nothing.

⁵*tu—valuisti* : " you had power enough not only to disregard the judicial trials, but also to subvert them and weaken their power." Distinguish *jus,* what the law ordains, or the obliga-tions it imposes, from *lex,* a written statute or ordinance. —*quaestiones :* the *praetor urbanus* and *praetor peregrinus* dispensed justice in private and less important cases. In case of any magnitude the people acted as jury themselves, or appointed one or more to preside at the trial. Those appointed were called *quaesitores* or *quaestores.* In 150 B.C. *four* permanent praetors were appointed to aid the *praetor urbanus* and *praetor* peregimus. One had charge of all cases of extortion ; another, of bribery ; another, of treason ; another, of frauds against the public treasury. These four classes of trials were called *quaes-tiones perpetuae.*

superiora : " former acts of yours."

⁶*nunc—ferendum* : " but now that I should be wholly on your account the slave of fear, that in every, even the least rumour, Catiline should be dreaded, that no plot seems possible to be entered into, in which your villany has no share (these things, I say), are not to be endured."—*totam* : fem : referring to *patriam.*

⁷*ne—opprimar* : scil. *discede, atque hunc mihi timorem eripe.*

CHAPTER VIII.

§ 19.—¹*impetrare*: "to obtain its request :" i.e. *ut ex urbe exeas.*

²*quid? quod*: see note 16, § 11.

³*in custodiam*: when a person of rank was suspected of any treasonable act, he generally surrendered himself into the hands of some responsible person, to be guarded until his guilt or innocence was established. This was called *custodia libera.*

· ⁴*apud M'*: another reading is *ad M.* The person was Manius (not Marcus) Lepidus who held the office of consulship with Volcatius Tullus B.C. 68.

domi meae: would *domi* with other adjectives be allowable?

⁵*isdem parietibus*: here the idea of *means* is combined with that of place : H. 425, II., 1.1).

qui—essem = quippe qui—essem: "inasmuch as I was in great danger."

quod—contineremur: when does *quod* take the indicative and when the subjunctive : H. 516, I., II. ?

⁶*sodalem*: "your boon companion :" distinguish *socius* (root *sec*, to follow, hence *sequor*), a follower : *consors*, a partner in lot : *comes*, a companion on a journey: *sodalis*, a boon companion.

⁷*virum optimum*: probably ironical : nothing is known of him, except that he was weak and simple.

⁸*videlicet* and *scilicet*: "no doubt :" both introduce an explanation with the difference, that the former generally indicates the true, the latter, the wrong explanation, though sometimes, as in the present passage, the meanings are reversed. Z. 345.

⁹*ad vindicandum* : "in bringing you to punishment."

a vinculis: the state prison which was used to detain prisoners, not for penal imprisonment in opposition to (*custodia libera*) private custody.

¹⁰*qui = quippe qui*: H., 517.

§ 20.—¹*quae cum ita sint* : see note.

²*emori*: another reading is *morari*, antithetical to *abire*.

³*refer ad senatum*: "bring up (the matter scil. *rem*) before the Senate."—*referre* is the technical term to express the laying of the subject for debate before the Senate, which was done by the consul or presiding magistrate : *deferee*, denotes the simple announcement of anything : *placere*, is the usual term to express the decision of the Senate. The aristocratic party had

advised Catiline to go into exile, preferring that he should take this course rather than that they should have an open conflict with him.

4sibi—decreverit : "shall decree by their vote." The senators voted "yea" or "nay" by saying *placet* or *non placet*.

5abhorret—moribus : "is inconsistent with my character." The fact is the Senate could not pass a sentence of exile.

6si—expectas : "if it is this word (exile) you are waiting for."

7patiuntur—tacent : i.e., they suffer me to use this bold language to you and still they raise no word on your behalf.

8quid—perspicis? "why do you wait for the sentence of these in words, where will you perceive, though they are silent?"

§ 21.—*1huic* : "who is present." P. Sestius Gallus was quaestor to the consul Antonius who as *tribunus plebis* in 57 B.C. was active for Cicero's recall from banishment. Cicero defended him in 56 B.C. in an action *de vi.*

2vim—intulisset : "would have laid violent hands on me:" a species of hendiadys. Even his dignity as consul, and the sacred shrine of Juppiter Stator would not have shielded him.

3quiescunt probant: patiuntur, decernunt : tacent, clamant: note these examples of *oxymoron.*

4cives, scil. *idem faciunt* i.e. *silentio probant.* The *equites* formed the second or middle order of the Roman State.

5prosequantur : those who went into voluntary exile were often accompanied to the gates by their friends. An escort is promised Catiline to express the delight in getting rid of him.

CHAPTER IX.

§ 22.—*1quamquam* : cp. καίτοι ; "and yet," used here as a corrective particle.

2te ; scil. *sperandumne sit fore ut* : "is it to be expected that anything will break your resolve?" Note the emphatic positions of *te, tu, tu, tu.* What feelings do these interrogations express?

3duint = dent : often used in religious formulas. Give the construction of *utinam* : H., 483, 1.

4animum induxeris : Cicero uses the form *animum inducere* (except in Pro Sulla, 30, 83) and Livy always *in animum inducere.*

4

⁵*quanta—impendeat*: "what a storm of unpopularity threatens me, if not at present, on account of the memory of your crimes being fresh, still in the future time." *recenti*=*memoria* : abl. of cause. *in posteritatem* = *in posterum tempus*. *impendeat* : indirect question.

⁶*sed—sejungatur* : "but (the unpopularity you threaten) willingly will I undergo (literally, pays me well) provided the loss which you forbode is confined to myself and does not involve danger to the State." *tanti* : genitive of price. The subject of *est* is *invidiam istam mihi impendere*.

⁷*ut—ut—ut* : these three clauses are explained by the three beginning with *aut, aut, aut*. *pudor* = αἰδώς ; "a sense of shame, or modesty."

§ 23.—¹*conflare* : a metaphor taken from metals : literally, "to smelt together : " hence "to heap upon."

²*recta*, scil, *via* : " straightway."

³*vix—vix*: note the emphatic positions : "hard will it be for me to bear the weight of the unpopularity caused by you, if you go into exile by the order of the consul,"—*sermones* : "the censure : " cp. our expression "to be the talk of the town." *feceris* : see note 4, § 6.

⁴*sui—mavis* : "but if, however, you prefer to consult my praise and glory." *laus—gloria* are originally derived from the same root CLU, "to hear : " *laus* = (c)*lau*(*d*)*s* : *gloria* = *clu-oria*.

⁵*exsulta—latrocinio* : "triumph in your impious bandit war." *latro*: properly a mercenary soldier who serves for pay (λατρεία) : afterwards, "a brigand." *impio* : as being against his native land : cp. *pietas erga patriam*, "patriotism."

§ 24.—¹*quamquam* : see note 1, § 22. *invitem* : rhetorical question : H. 529.

²*qui—armati?* "to wait for you arms near Forum Amelium." *ad* before the name of towns denotes (1) direction ; (2) proximity, as in this passage. Towns were called *Fora*, by the Romans, where the praetor held his circuits for administering justice and where markets were established. The town mentioned here was in Etruria between the Armenta (*Fiora*) and Marta, not from the sea. It is now called *Monte Alto*. It derived its name from one Aurelius, who built the *Via Aurelia* from Rome to Pisa.

praestolarentur : the word *praestolari*, is "to wait for" said of a subordinate who performs some services for a superior.

[3]*pactam—diem* : from what verb is *pactam* ?—*dies*, in the sense of a "fixed day" is usually feminine.

[4]*aquilam* : the same that Marius carried in his Cimbric war. Catiline fell beside it at Pistoria (Gall. Cat. C. 59). A silver eagle with extended wings, and on the top of a spear was the ensign of the whole legion. The *signa* were the standards of the *manipuli* and the *vexillum* is the standard of the cavalry.

[5]*cui—fuit* : "for which the secret place where you concocted your crimes was prepared in your house." The eagle was usually kept in a part of the *praetorium* which was consecrated (*sacrarium*).

[6]*tu—solebas* : scil. *credendumne sit fore* : "is it to be believed that you could any longer be without this, to which you when setting out to slaughter were wont to pay your vows?"

[7]*alturibus* : only plural in classical Latin.

CHAPTER X.

§ 25.—[1]*haec res* : i.e. *hoc bellum contra patriam, haec civium caedes.*

[2]*quandam—voluptatem* : "a kind of delight, (really) inconceivable."

[3]*ad—servavit* : "it was for this mad career that nature gave you being, inclination trained you, fate reserved you :" distinguish *amentia*, and *dementia*.

[4]*non modo*, for the omission of *non* after *non modo*, see Madvig., § 461, C. When the sentence is negative, *non modo* = *non modo non*, the second *non* being omitted, if both sentences have the same verb, and if the verb is contained in the second sentence, for the negative is thus considered to belong conjointly to both sentences. Z. 724, b.

[5]*otium* : "peace," opposed to *bellum.*

[6]*nefarium* : "unhallowed," as involving *impietas contra patriam.*

[7]*nanctus es* : "you have got together."—The orator is *atque* (ex) *derelictis ab non modo omni fortuna, rerum etiam* (a) *spe.*

[8]*conflatam* : a metaphor taken from metals, "smelted together," hence "collected."

§ 26.—[1]*hic* : i.e. *inter ejusmodi hominum gregem.*—*qua—perfruere* : "what gratification will you experience." Notice the climax in this sentence.

[2]*ad—tui* : " it was for the earnest prosecution of this life that these feats of endurance, which are made so much of, were practised."—*meditari* : is used passively : as *abominatus, amplexus, confessus, detestatus, dimensus, exsecratus, moderatus, suetus.* M. 153. Wit^h *meditari* : cp. μελεᾶν.

[3]*ad—strupium* : " to watch for an opportunity to commit an act of debauchery." = *ad tempus stupro opportunum observandum.* The infinitive clauses *jacere, vigilare,* are in opposition with *labores.*

[4]*ad—obeundum :* " to execute some daring deed."

[5]*otiosorum*: " the peaceable citizens." Another reading is *occisorum.*

[6]*habes—omnium :* " you have (now) an opportunity of showing the renowned endurance you have for withstanding hunger, cold, (and) a need of all things :" cp. Sallust, Cat. C., 5 : *corpus potiens inediae, vigiliae, algoris, supra quam unquam credibile est.*

[7]*quibus* : to be referred to *famis, frigoris, inopiae,* not to *omnium rerum.*

§ 27.—[1]*tantum confeci* : " this much, I gained."

[2]*quum—reppuli* : at the last election, Cicero adopted these measures especially aimed at Catiline : a bill to increase the penalty against bribery *(ambitus) ;* by disarranging the plans of Catiline in putting off the elections, and appearing in the Campus Martius in armour.

[3]*exul—consul : latrocinium—bellum :* note the *paronomasia.*

CHAPTER XI.

[4]*.letester ac?deprecer :* both these words mean " to seek to remove anything from one, such as blame, &c., by calling the gods to witness *(testari deos)* and by imploring *(precari)* their aid. Note the middle force of these deponents.

[5]*praeso :* conjugate this verb.

[6]*loquatur :* see § 18.

[7]*tunc* : join with *exire patiere.*

[8]*evoratorum servorum :* Catiline, however, refused the help of slaves (Sallust, Cat. C., 56), though Lentulus urged him to use these.

[9]*emissus—immissus* : paronomasia.

[10]*hunc—duci* : what is the usual construction of *imperari ?* H, 498, 1. The infinitive with *imperare* is always passive.

[11]*mactari* : the official word of sacrifice, " to slay a victim." It is connected with old verb *magere :* probably " to strike :" cp. μάχη, hence " to kill."

§ 28.—[1]*tandem* : cp. note 1, § 1. Cicero shews that neither precedent, nor laws, nor the judgment of future generations deter Catiline.

[2]*At* : introduces the objection of an opponent : " Yes, but.'' Cicero refers here to the case of P. Scipio Nasica who headed the nobility against Tib. Gracchus.

[3]*au leges ?* Principally the *leges Valeriae* and *leges Porciae.* The former were proposed by (1) P. Valerius Poplicola 509 B.C. which enacted that no Roman magistrate should put to death or flog a Roman citizen if he had appealed to the people : (2) in 449 B.C. L. Valerius Potitus enacted that no magistracy should be held with an exemption from appeal : (3) in 300 B.C. M. Valerius Corvus brought in a bill sanctioning the other laws on the subject of appeal. The *leges Porciae* were proposed by three of the *Porcii*, and exempted from stripes the persons of Roman citizens, and imposed heavy fines on any one who should scourge or kill a Roman citizen.

[4]*rogatae sunt* : " have been passed." The people at the *comitia* were *asked* to pass a law by the presiding magistrate in the words "*velitis, jubeatis, Quirites.*" Hence *rogare legem,* " to pass a bill." When the people voted *two* ballots were usually given them, one marked with the letters U R (i.e. *uti rogas* or " yea "), and the other with A (i.e. *antiquo, antiqua probo,* " I annul ").

[5]*praeclaram gratiam* : " a fine return :" strongly ironical.

[6]*hominem—cognitum* : i.e. *hominem novum* : the Romans applied the term (*novus homo*) to the first of a family who had raised himself to a consul office. *tam mature* : the *lex annalis* enacted that no one could obtain the *quaestorship* till he was 31 ; the *aedileship* till 37 ; the *praetorship* till 41 ; and the *consulship* till 43. Cicero means that he obtained these offices as soon as he was eligible to hold them.

[7]*propter invidiam* : " because of too disquieting fear of un-popularity."

§ 29.—[1]*num—pertimescenda ?* " Is the ill-will arising from a strict and a firm discharge of duty to be feared rather than that arising from indolence and indifference."

50 NOTES.

CHAPTER XII.

²actu : give rules for the use of the supines : H. 547.

³judicarem : this tense in the *protasis* with the plupf. in the *apo losis*, denotes that the action is going on simultaneously.

⁴unius—horae : "the enjoyment of a single hour." *Usura* : properly "interest" paid for the *use* of capital.

⁵gladiatori isti : contemptuously.

⁶etenim : "and (well may I make this assertion), for :" cp. καὶ γάρ.

⁷summi viri : referred to the *magistratus; clarissimi cives*, to the *viri privati*.

⁸honestarunt = decoraverunt : "graced."

§ 30.—*¹quamquam = καίτοι*, corrective : "and yet."

²qui—dissimulent : "of such a character that they either are blind to those evils which threaten us, or profess blindness in regard to the things they see." *Qui = tales ut* : H. 501 : this explains this subjunctive.

³qui—aluerunt=hi—aluerunt : not to be connected with *non-nulli sunt*, as this would require *aluerint*.

⁴si—animadvertissem : "if I had punished him," : with such a meaning understand *supplicio* : the preposition *in* is necessary when the meaning is "to punish with an authoritative and steady hand." *regie* : "in a tyrannical manner."

⁵pervenerit : fut. perf.

⁶paulisper—posse : "may for a season be repressed, but can-for ever be suppressed" ; *reprimo* : to hold in check merely for a short time ; *comprimo* : to completely check.

⁷se ejecerit scil, *ex urbe*.

⁸ceteros naufragos : "the rest of his shipwrecked band of followers" : i.e., shipwrecked in character and fortune by reason of their excesses.

⁹tam adulta pestis : "this fully developed plague-poison" : *adulta :* from root *ul, ol, al,* "high."

CHAPTER XIII.

§ 31.—*¹jamdia* : for the space of three years from the consulate of Lepidus and Tullus, 66 B.C. ; *nescio quo pacto* : "in some way or other" : literally, "I know not on what terms " : cp. οἰκ οἶδα οντινα τρόπον, *nescio quo modo.*

[2]*omnium—erupit* : a pregnant construction as if he had meant :
" all these crimes have been a-ripening up to, and the continued
career of frenzy and boldness have burst forth in, the time of my
consulship." The metaphor is probably borrowed from an ulcer,
bursting when ripe.

[3]*ex tanto latrocinio=ex tot latronum numero, latrocinium =
latrones,* cp. *servitium=servi : conjuratio=conjurati—residebit :*
the metaphor is taken from a subtle poison in the system. The
state is looked upon by the orator as the body, the conspiracy as
the fever, and the execution of Catiline as the draught of cool
water which momentarily refreshes.

[4]*visceribus* : *viscera* were the upper vitals, including the heart,
lungs, liver, &c : *intestina,* were the liver vitals. Observe the
force of *atque* and the repetition of the preposition.

[5]*cum—jactantur :* there is no hendiadys here, but merely an
accumulation of synonymous terms. Observe the middle force
of *jactantur* : "toss themselves about."

[6]*biberint :* Madvig reads *biberunt.*

[7]*qui est :* "which exists."—*relevatus :* "mitigated."

[8]*vehementius—ingravescet* : "shall become more chronic if
the others are allowed to live" : *vivis reliquis* : abl. abs.

§ 32.—[1]*prætoris urbani :* L. Valerius Flaccus was *Prætor
Urbanus* at this time, and the partisans of Catiline thronged
around his *tribunal* to intimidate him when delivering judgment
in cases of debt.

[2]*obsidēre—curiam* : "to beset the senate house in arms."
Romulus divided the people into three tribes (*tribus*) and each
tribe was divided into ten wards (*curiæ*). Each *curia* had a
temple for the performance of its religious rites and for holding
political meetings : the root is *cur :* "to be powerful ;" cp.
Quirites, hence, "the powerful men" : κύριος, κοίρανος.—*cum
gladiis = armati.*

[3]*malleolos* : properly *malleolus,* is "a hammer," the tranverse
head of which was formed for holding pitch and tow. These
latter were set on fire and thrown slowly that they might not be
extinguished, to ignite houses and other buildings. Translate
" fire-darts."

[4]*quid—sentiat* : "what his sentiments are respecting the state: "
dep. quest.—*polliceor—fore* : what verbs are construed with the
future infinitive ?

[5]*patefacta—oppressa* : note the balancing of these words, and
the asyndeton.

§ 33.—¹*hisce ominibus:* "with these prophetic words" : a kind of abl. absolute.

²*cum—exitio* : with the best interests of the republic (fully established), and with your own calamity and ruin (fully assured) and with the destruction of these" : *cum* here denotes an accompanying circumstance as a result or consequence of an action: z, **472.**

³*tu* : addressing the statue of Juppiter in the temple of Juppiter Stator.

⁴*auspiciis* : not only temples but also statues were consecrated, by taking auspices.

⁵*statorem* : " the flight staying ": see note 6, § **11.** A kind of rhetorical exaggeration,' as the temple was only viewed by Romulus and built much later ; Livy x. **37.**

⁶*arcebis* : with a softened imperative force : so also *mactabis*

PROPER NAMES.

A

Ahāla, -ae : m.: *Caius Servilius Ahala* was master of the horse to the dictator Cincinnatus, 439 B.C. Spurius Maelius, one of the *Equites*, bought corn at a low rate and distributed it gratuitiously to the poor. By this he gained the favour of the plebeians, but incurred the enmity of the patricians. When he was summoned by the dictator to appear on the charge of aiming at royal power, he refused, and Ahala, with an armed band, rushed into the crowd where he was standing, and slew him. Cicero often praises the deed of Ahala, but it is doubtful whether it can be defended.

E

Etrūrĭa, -ae : f.: a large district of Italy, lying west and north of the Tiber. This part of Italy was generally favorable to Catiline. In it were *Faesulae*, and *Pistoria*, where Catiline fell, 62 B.C.

F

Faesulae, ārum : f.: now *Fiesole*, near Florentia (*Florence*), in Etruria. Here Catiline raised the standard of rebellion.

Fŏrum Aurēlĭum, Fŏri Aurēlĭi : n.: a town of Etruria, on the Aurelian way ; now *Monte Alto.*

Flaccus, -i : m.: *M. Fulvius Flaccus* was charged with the execution of the Agrarian law of the Gracchi, and aided Tib. Gracchus to gain for all the Italians the rights of Roman citizenship. He was cited along with the consul Opimius to render an account of his conduct with regard to the revolutionary measures then proposed. This he refused to obey, and was slain along with his eldest son.

Fulvius, -i : m.: see preceding.

G

Gracchus, -i : m.: *Tiberius Sempronius Gracchus* and *Caius Sempronius Gracchus* were sons of Tiberius Sempronius Gracchus and of Cornelia, daughter of Scipio Africanus Major. The object of both brothers was to have the public lands divided and given to the poor, by allowing no one to hold more than 500 *jugera* of land. The state was to compensate the wealthy for all the loss. Both brothers fell in the sedition that arose out of their revolutionary schemes : Tiberius in 132 B.C., and Caius in 122 B.C.

I

Itălĭa, -ae : f.: Italy, a country of Southern Europe.

J

Jānŭārĭus, -a, -um : adj.: of or belonging to *January*.

Juppĭter, Jŏvis : m.: Juppiter, the supreme god of Roman mythology.

L

Laeca, -ae : m.: *M. Porcius Laeca*, an accomplice of Catiline, who convened at his house the leading members of the conspiracy.

Lēpĭdus, -i : m.: *M'. Lepidus*, consul with L. Volcatius Tullus 67 B.C.

Lēpĭdus, -i : m.: *M. Lepidus*, consul with Catulus 79 B.C.

M

Maelĭus, -i : m.: *Spurius Maelius*, a Roman *Eques*, who attempted to gain regal power at Rome by securing the favour of the plebeians 449 B.C. This he tried to do by supplying corn at a low rate. He was summoned to appear before Cincinnatus, the dictator, but refused, and was slain by Ahala.

Manliānus, -a, -um : adj.: of or belonging to Manlius.

Manlĭus, -i : m.: *Caius Manlius*, an accomplice of Catiline, and sent to Etruria to collect troops. He commanded the right wing of Catiline's army at Pistoria, and "foremost fighting fell."

Marcellus, -i : m.: *Marcus Marcellus*, an accomplice and intimate friend of Catiline.

Mětellus, -i : m.: *Q. Caecilius Metellus Celer*, praetor in 63 B.C. He was despatched by Cicero into the Gallic and Picene districts to raise a force against Catiline. He was consul 61 B.C., and poisoned by his wife Clodia 59 B.C.

N

Nŏvembris, -e : adj.: belonging to November.

O

Opĭmĭus, -i : m.: *Lucius Opimius* was consul in 122 B.C. He opposed the designs of C. Gracchus.

P

Pălātĭum, -i : n.: the Palatine hill was the largest of the seven hills on which Rome was built. Romulus laid here the foundation of the city, and here in the imperial period were the residences of the Roman emperors.

Praeneste, -is : n.: now *Palestrina*, an ancient city of Latium, 23 miles S.E. of Rome. Its citadel was remarkable for the strength of its position.

R

Rōma, -ae : f.: Rome, a celebrated town on the Tiber.

Rōmānus, -a, -um : adj.: of or belonging to Rome : *Roman*.

Rōmŭlus, -i : m.: the founder of Rome and king of the city from 753–715 B.C.

S

Sāturnīnu3, -ĭ: m.: *L. Saturninus*, a tribune of the people and a violent partisan of Marius, who abetted him in his numerous misdeeds. He is said to have caused the death of C. Memmius 102 B.C. At length, after many cruel acts, the people became aroused against him, and he was slain in the forum.

Scīpĭo, -ōnĭs: m.: *P. Cornelius Scipio Nasica* was consul 138 B.C. His character was held in the highest estimation by his countrymen. He opposed the measures of Gracchi. After the death of Tiberius Gracchus, unpopularity overtook Scipio, and he was sent to Asia, where he died of chagrin.

Servilius, -ĭ: m.: *C. Servilius Glaucia*, a seditious and profligate individual, put to death 121 B.C.

Stator: "the flight staying:" an epithet of Juppiter.

T

Tullĭus, -ĭ: m.: *M. Tullius Cicero.* See Introduction.

Tullus, -ĭ: m.: See *M'. Lepidus.*

V

Vălērĭus, -ĭ: m.: *L. Valerius.* a partner of Marius in the consulship, 121 B.C.

ABBREVIATIONS.

a., *or* act.	active.
abl.	ablative.
acc.	accusative
adj.	adjective.
adv.	adverb.
cp.	compare.
com. gen.	common gender.
comp.	comparative degree
conj.	conjunction.
dat.	dative.
def.	defective.
dem.	demonstrative.
dep.	deponent.
dim.	diminutive.
f.	feminine.
fr.	from.
fut.	future.
freq.	frequentative.
gen.	genitive.
Gr.	Greek.
imperat.	imperative.
impers.	impersonal.
inc.	inceptive.
inch.	inchoative.
ind.	indicative.
indecl.	indeclinable.
indef.	indefinite.
inf.	infinitive.
intens.	intensive.
interj.	interjection.
interrog.	interrogative.
m.	masculine.
n.	neuter.
nom.	nominative.
num.	numeral.
part.	participle.
pa.	participal adjective
pass.	passive.
perf.	perfect.
pl.	plural.
pluperf.	pluperfect.
pos.	positive degree.
poss.	possessive.
prep.	preposition.
pres.	present.
pret.	preteritive.
pron.	pronoun.
rel.	relative.
semi-dep.	semi-deponent.
sing.	singular.
subj.	subjunctive.
sup.	superlative degree.
voc.	vocative.
=	equal to.

N.B.—Where the etymology is not given, the word is of very uncertain or unknown origin.

VOCABULARY.

A

ā, ab, abs, prep. with abl. (a, only before consonants; ab, before vowels and consonants). *From, away from; by* [akin to Gr. ἀπ·ό].

ab-eo, īre, ĭi, ĭtum, v. n. [ab, "away;" ĕo, "to go"] *To go away, depart.*

ab-horreo, horruĭ, no sup., horrēre, n. and a. [ab, "from;" horreo, "to dread"] *To be averse or disinclined to; to be free from.*

ab-sum, esse, fuĭ, n. irreg. *To be away from; to be absent.*

ab-ūtor, ūsus sum, utĭ, dep. n. [ab, "away from," hence "wrongly;" utor, "I use"] *To misuse, abuse.*

ac, conj. (used before consonants). *And.*

ācer, ācris, ācre, adj. [AC, "to sharpen"] *Sharp, severe.*

āc-erb-us, a, um, adj. (ac-er) *Unripe, sour; violent.*

āc-ĭes, ĭĕi, f. (ac-er) *An edge, point.*

ācr-ĭter, adv. (ācer) *Strongly, sharply, keenly.*

ad, prep. with acc. Locally : a, *To, towards.*—(b) *Before* a place.— *Up to* a certain time.—With Gerunds or Gerundives : *For, for the purposes of.*

ad-dūco, duxi, ductum, dūcĕre, a. [ad, "to;" duco, "I lead"] *To lead to; induce, lead.*

ad-eo, adv. *So far; so long; so much.*

ad-fero, ferre, attuli, allātum, irr. a. (ad ; fero) *To bring to, bring.*

adflic-to, tāvi, tātum, tāre, a., intens. (for adflig-to, fr. adflig-o). *To greatly trouble, harass, annoy.*

ad-grego : see aggrego.

ad-hibeo, hibuĭ, hibitum, hĭbēre, a. (ad ; habeo) *To apply to; to use, employ.*

ad-huc, adv. *Thus far, up to this time.*

ad-minister, tri, m. [ad, "to;" ministro, "to serve"] *A servant, assistant.*

ad-miror, mĭratus sum ; mĭrari [ad, "to;" miror, "to wonder at"] dep. *To wonder at, admire.*

ad-sĕquor, secūtus (quūtus), sequi, dep. a. *To follow, pursue.*

ad-servo, servāvi, servātum, servāre [ad, "to;" servo, "to keep"] *To preserve, protect.*

ad-sĭdĕo, sēdi, sessum, sĭdĕre [ad, "near;" sedeo, "to sit"] n. (ad ; sedeo) *To sit by or near.*

ădŭlesc-ens, entis, m. and f. [ad, "to;" ŏlesco, "to grow;" the root assumes the form of AL, OL, UL, in Latin as *altus, sub-oles, adultus*] *A young man* (from the 15th or 17th until past the 30th year).

ădŭlescent-ulus, i, m., dim. (adulescens) *A youn man ; stripling.*

ădul-tus, a, um, part. (adol-esco) *Grown up, adult, full-grown.*

adven-tus, ūs, m. [ad, "to;" venio, "to come"] *A coming, arrival.*

aeger, gra, grum, adj. *Weak, sick.*

aequus, a, um, adj. [root II, "to make even :" cp. aequor] *Plain, smooth, even ; aequo animo, with great composure.*

aes-tus, ūs, m. [for aed-tus : roct AED, "to burn :" cp. aestas ; αἴθω] *Heat.*

aet-ernus, a, um, adj. [for ae (vi) ternus : root AIV, a lengthened form of I, "to go;" cp. αἰών] *Eternal, everlasting.*

ag-grĕgo, grĕgāvi, grĕgātum, gregare, v. a. [ad ; grex, *to lead to a flock*] *To assemble, collect together.*

a-gnosco, gnóvi, gnítum, gnoscčre, a. (for ad-gnosco, gnosco = nosco) *To recognize, to discern.*

ăgo, ēgi, actum, ăgěre [AG, "to set in motion"] a. *To drive; to do, perform, effect; to treat; plead.*

aio, def. [root AGH, "to say"] *To speak; to say "yes;" to affirm.*

ălĭ-ēnus, a, um, adj. (ali-us, belonging to the) *Belonging to another, foreign; unfriendly.*

ălĭqu-ando, adv. (aliquis, *of time, past, future, and present. At some time or other; at length.*

ălĭ-qui, qua, quod, indef. pron. adj. (ali-us; qui) *Some, any.*

ălĭquid, adv. (adverbial neut. acc. of aliquis) *In some degree, somewhat.*

ălĭ-quis, aliquid [fem. sing. and fem. and neut. plur. not used; alius; quis, root AL, "another:" cp. alter, ἄλλος: Eng. else], indef. pron. subst. *Some one, any one; something.*

ălĭquo, adv. (adverbial abl. of aliquis) *Some whither, to some place.*

ălĭ-quot, indef. num. adj., indecl. (alius; quot) *Some, several.*

ălĭus a, ud, adj. (gen. sing. alīus, dat. alii) *Another, other; alius . . alius, one . . . another.*

ălo, ălŭi, ălĭtum, or altum, alěre, a. *To nourish; to foster.*

altārĭa, ĭum, n. (alt-um, things pertaining to the; hence) *An altar.*

āmentĭa, ae, f. [a, prio, mens, "mind"] *Madness.*

ăm-īcus, i, m. (amo) *A friend.*

ampl-ĭus, comp. adv. *More; longer.*

am-plus, a, um, adj. [am = ambi, "around;" root PLE, "to fill;" hence plebs, pleo, plenus] *Abundant, full; illustrious, noble.*

an, conj. *Or, whether.*

ănĭm-adverto, verti, versum, advertěre, a. (animus; adverto) *To attend to; to consider, perceive; animadvertere in aliquem, to inflict punishment on one.*

ănĭmus, i, m. [root AU, "to breathe"] *The mind; disposition; thought.*

annus, i, m. [perhaps for amnus: root AM, "to go round"] *A year.*

ante, prep. with acc. *Before, in front of; as adverb, before, previously.*

ant-ĭquus, a, um, adj. [ant-e, "before"] *Ancient, old.*

ăperte, adv. (apertus) *Openly.*

ăpud, prep. with acc. (obs. apo, to seize) *Near, at, by; with.*

ăqua, ae, f. *Water.*

ăquĭla, ae, f. [AC, "sharp," or "swift"] *The eagle; the standard of the legion.*

arbĭtr-or, ātus sum, ari, v. dep. a. [ar = ad, "to;" bito, "to go:" hence one who approaches a cause to enquire into it] *To judge, think.*

arcĕo, arcŭi, no. sup., arcěre [root ARC, "to protect:" cp. arceus, ἀρκεῖν] a. *To shut up; to keep or hold off.*

ardĕo, arsi, arsum, ardēre, n. *To burn, blaze.*

argent-ĕus, a, um, adj. (argentum, pertaining to) *Of silver.*

arma, ōrum, n. pl. [root AR, "to fit:" hence all things fitted on] *Arms, weapons.*

armā-tus, i, m. *An armed man, a soldier.*

arm-o, āvi, ātum, āre. *To furnish with arms; to arm.*

aspec-tus, tūs, m. (aspic-io) *A seeing, sight.*

a+ [old form ast: cp. ἀτ-άρ], conj. *But, yet (to introduce a reason for a supposed objection), but certainly, but consider.*

atque or ăc (the latter only before consonants), conj. *And also, and especially.*

ātrox, ōcis, [a, ĭntens.: trux, "cruel"] adj. *Horrid, terrible, frightful.*

at-tendo (3), tendi, tentum, a. (ad; tendo) *To apply the mind to; to consider.*

auctor, ōris, m. (augeo) *An author, contriver.*

auctōrĭtas, ātis, f. (auctor) *Authority.*

audă-cia, ae, f. (audax, the quality of the) *Audacity, insolence.*

audĕo, ausus sum, audĕre, semidep. *To dare.*

audio, audīvi, audītum, audīre [AV, "to hear"] a. *To hear.*

aur-is, is, f. (audio, *the hearing thing*) *The ear.*

auspic-ium, ii, n. (auspex, *a bird inspector, diviner*, one who marks the flight and cries of birds, and then gives predictions] *Augury from birds, auspices.*

aut, conj. *Or;* aut . . . aut, *either . . . or.*

autem, conj. *But, moreover.*

avus [AV, "to hear," hence "to obey," cp. obedio], i, m. *A grandfather.*

B

bacch-or (1), dep. n. (Bacch-us) *To revel.*

b-ellum (old form du-ellum), i, n. (duo, *a contest between two parties*) *War, warfare.*

bibo, bibi, no sup., bibĕre [root PO, "to drink:" cp. poto, πίνω], a. *To drink.*

bonum, i, n. *A good thing;* in pl., *goods.*

bonus, a, um, adj. (comp. melior, sup. optimus) *Good, well-disposed.*

brevis, e, adj. [root FRAG, "to break"] *Little, small, short.*

C

caedes, is, f. [root CAD, "to fall:" cp. cado] *Slaughter.*

caelum, i, n. [for cavillum; fr. cavus, "hollow"] *Heaven.*

calamitas, ātis, f. [for cadamitas; root CAD, "to fall"] *Loss, calamity, disaster.*

campus, i, m. [root SCAP, "to dig:" cp. κῆπος] *A plain, field.*

capio, cēpi, captum, capĕre [root CAP, "to hold"] a. *To take;* consilium capere, *to form a plan.*

carcer, ĕris, m. [root ARC, "to enclose:" cp. ark] *A prison.*

careo, ŭi, ĭtum, ēre, n. *To be without.*

carus, a, um, adj. [for camrus : cam, "to love:" amare = (c)amare] *Dear, precious.*

castrum, i, n. [for scadtrum; SCAD, "to cover:" Eng. shed] *A castle, fort;* in pl., castra, ōrum, n., *a camp.*

ca-sus, sūs, um. (for cad-sus, fr. cad-o, "to fall") *Accident, chance.*

causa, ae, f. *A cause, reason.*

cedo, cessi, cessum, cēdĕre, n. *To go; to yield.*

certe, adv. (certus) *Certainly.*

cer-tus, a, um, adj. (cer-no) *Decided, fixed, definite.*

ceterus, a, um (the nom. sing. mas. not in use), adj. *The other, the rest, the remainder.*

circum-cludo, clūsi, clūsum, clūdĕre (circum ; claudo). *To shut in, enclose.*

circum-sto, steti, no sup., stāre, n. or a. *To stand around.*

civis, is, com. gen. [root CI, "to lie," or "dwell:" hence "a dweller"] *A citizen.*

civ-itas, ātis, f. (id., the condition or state of the; gen. pl., ium and um) *Citizenship; a state.*

clamo, clāmāvi, clāmātum, clāmāre [root CAL, "to shout"] n. and a. *To call, shout aloud.*

clarus, a, um, adj. [root KAL. "to call"] *Clear, renowned.*

cle-mens, mentis, adj. (clino, *to bend;* mens, *having the heart bent*) *Mild, kind.*

coepi, coepisse, a, or n. def. (contracted fr. co-apio, fr. con ; apo, *to seize*) *To begin.*

co-erceo, ui, itum, ercere, a. (con ; arceo, *to shut up*) *To surround, restrain, check.*

coe-tus, tūs, m. [con, "together:" eo, "to go"] *A coming together; an assemblage, company.*

co-gito, gitāvi, gitātum, gitāre [co = con, "together:" agito, "to set in motion"] *To weigh thoroughly in the mind; to think over; reflect upon; plan.*

co-gnosco, gnōvi, gnitum, gnoscĕre, a. [co (= cum), in augmentative sense ; gnosco = nosco, " to become acquainted with "] *To know*.

col-ligo, lēgi, lectum, ligĕre [col (= cum), in an augmentative sense; [ego, "to gather"] *To gather or collect together*.

col-loco, a. (con ; loco) *To lay, place*.

cŏlōn-ĭa, ae, f. [root COL, "to till ;" cp. colo] *A colony, settlement*.

cŏm-e-s, ĭtis, com. gen. (con; eo, *one who goes with another*) *A companion*.

cŏm-ĭ-tĭum, ii, n. (con ; i, root of eo, *a coming together*) *The Comitium*, i.e. the place where the Romans assembled to vote ; in pl., *the comitia*, i.e. *the assembly itself*, hence *election*.

commendẝtĭo, tĭōnis, f. (commend[a]-o) *A recommendation, praise*.

com-mitto, mĭsi, missum, mittĕre, a. (con ; mitto, *to cause to go together*) *To commit*. ...

com-mŏvĕo, mōvi, mōtum, mŏvĕre, a. (con ; moveo) *To move, rouse*.

com-mūnis, e, adj. [com = cum munis, "serving"] *Common, general*.

com-păro, părāvi, părātum, părāri, v. a. [com = cum ; paro, "to prepare"] *To make rēady*..

com-pĕrio, pĕri, pertum, perīre, a. (cum ; root per, akin to perior, *to go through*) *To discover*.

compĕt-ītor, ōris, m. [com = bum ; peto, "to seek ;" hence to seek office] *A rival, competitor*.

com-plūres, a, and ia, adj. (con ; plus) *Several together, very many*.

com-prĕhendo, prĕhendi, prĕhensum, prehendere [com = cum ; intensive: prehendo, "to seize"] *To lay hold of, arrest*.

com-prīmo, pressi, pressum, prīmĕre, a. (con ; premo) *To press together ; to hinder, check*.

cōnā-tus, tūs, m. *An attempt*.

con-cēdo, cessi, cessum, cēdĕre, n. or a. *To depart, withdraw*.

conci-to, tāvi, tātum. tāre, a. intens. (conci-eo, *to urge*) *To rouse up, excite*.

can-cŭpĭ-sco, cŭpīvi or cŭpii, cŭp-itum, cŭpiscĕre, a. inch. (con ; cupi-o) *To be very desirous of ; to long for*.

concur-sus, sūs, m. [for concurr-sus, fr. concurr-o, the action of) *A running, flocking together ; a concourse*.

con-demno, demnāvi, demnātum, demnāre, v. a. [con = cum, intensive ; damnum, "loss"] a. (con ; damno) *To condemn*.

con-fĕro, ferre, tŭli, lātum, a. [con = cum, intensive ; fero, "to bring" or "bear"] *To bring ; to carry ; to direct ; to arrange*.

confes-tim, adv. *Immediately*.

con-ficio, fēci, fectum, fĭcĕre, a. (con ; facio) *To prepare, complete ; to exhaust*.

con-fido, fīsus sum, fīdĕre, n. or a. semi-dep. *To trust ; to believe certainly*.

con-firmo, firmāvi, firmātum, firmāre. *To strengthen ; t assure*.

con-flăgro, flăgrāvi, flăgrātum, flăgrāre [con = cum, in an augmentative ; FLAG, "to burn ;" cp. flamma (= flag-ma)] *To be on fire, to burn up*.

con-flo, flāre, flāvi, flātum. *To blow together, kindle ; to excite*.

con-grĕgo, grĕgāvi, grĕgātum, grĕgāre, a. (con ; grex) *To flock together, assemble, unite*.

con-jĭcĭo, jēci, jectum, jĭcĕre, a. (con ; jacio) *To hurl, send, cast*.

con-jungo, junxi, junctum, jungĕre, a. *To join together, unite, associate*.

conjūrā-tĭo, ōnis, f. (co jūr[a]-o, the action of) *An agreement ; conspiracy, plot*.

conjūrā-tus, m. (id.) *A conspirator*.

conl : see coll.

cōnor, ātus sum, āri, dep. *To undertake, attempt*.

consciĕntĭa, ae, f. (conscien= conscious) *Consciousness, knowledg*

con-scrībo, scripsi, scriptum. scrībĕre, a. *To write together (in a list) ; to enroll*.

conscrip-tus, a, um, part. (for scrib-tus, fr. conscrib-o) As noun, m. (sc. pater) *a senator;* patres conscripti, *the old senators together with those who were afterwards admitted* (enrolled) *into its ranks;* originally, patres et conscripti, *senators.*

consen-sio, ōnis, f. (con-sentio) *Unanimity, agreement.*

consensus, ūs, m. [Id.] *Unanimity, agreement.*

con-servo, servāvi, servātum, servāre, a. *To preserve.*

consilium, ii, n. *Deliberation, counsel; plan, purpose; council.*

con-spicio, spexi, spectum, spicĕre, a. (con; specio, *to look*) *To observe, behold.*

con-stituo, stitŭi, stitūtum, stitŭere, a. (con; statuo) *To place; to erect; to arrange, settle, agree upon; to appoint.*

con-stringo, strinxi, strictum, stringĕre, a. *To draw, bind together; to hold, hold fast.*

consul, ūlis, m. *A consul,* one of the two chief magistrates of the Roman state, chosen yearly after the expulsion of the kings.

consul-āris, e, adj. (consul) *Of or pertaining to a consul; consular;* as noun, m., *ex-consul; one of the rank of consul.*

consul-ātus, ūs, m. (consul) *The consulship.*

consul-o, ŭi, tum, ĕre, n. or a. *To consider, consult;* consulere alicui, *to take counsel for some one;* consulere aliquem, *to ask the advice of some one.*

consul-tum, i, n. (con-sulo) *A decree, decision.*

con-tā-mino, a. (for con-tag-mino; fr. con; tag, root of tango) *To defile, contaminate.*

conten-tus, a, um, part. (con-tineo) *Contented, satisfied.*

con-tineo, tinŭi, tentum, tinĕre, a. (con; tene) *To hold together; to keep in, restrain, confine.*

con-tingo, tĭgi, tactum, tingĕre, a. (con; tango) *To touch, take hold of; to happen.*

contrā, adv. and prep. with acc. *Against, contrary to.*

contumēl-ia, ae, f. (obsolete contumēl-us, *swelling greatly*) *Abuse, insult, disgrace; reproach.*

con-venio, vēni, ventum, venire, n. or a. *To assemble;* used impersonally, *it is suitable, proper.*

con-vinco, vīci, victum, vincĕre, a. *To convict.*

con-voco, vocāvi, vocātum, vocāre, a. [con, "together;" voco, "to call"] *To convoke, assemble.*

cō-p-ia, ae, f. (contracted fr. co-op ia, fr. con; ops) *Abundance; wealth, riches; forces, troops* (generally in plural with the latter two meanings).

corpus, ŏris, n. *A body, corpse.*

cor-rigo, rexi, rectum, rigĕre, a. (con; rego) *To make straight; to improve, correct.*

cor-rōboro, a. (con; rōbŏro, *to strengthen*) *To strengthen; to corroborate, support.*

corrupt-ēla, ae, f. (corru[m]po) *That which corrupts; a corruption, seduction: seductive arts.*

cot-i-dīē, adv. (quot; (i); die, abl. of dies) *Daily.*

crēdo, dĭdi, dĭtum, crēdĕre, n. or a. *To trust in, believe; to think, suppose.*

cresco, crēvi, crētum, crescĕre, n. [root CRE, "to make grow;" cp. creo] *To grow, increase.*

crūdēli-ter, adv. (crudēlis, cruel) *Cruelly.*

cum, prep. with abl. *With.*

cum. *When, since, though.*

cŭmul-o, a. (cumul-us) *To accumulate; to complete; to increase.*

cunctus, a, um, adj. (contracted from conjunctus) *The whole, all.*

cupid-itas, ātis, f. (cupidus) *Desire; passion; eagerness; avarice.*

cŭp-ĭdus, a, um, adj. (cup-io) *Longing, desirous.*

cŭpio, ivi or ii, itum, cŭpĕre, a. and n. *To long for, desire.*

cur, adv. *Why?*

cur-a, ae, f. (for caer-a, fr. caero, old form of quaero) *Trouble, care.*

5

cūrĭa, ae, f. [root CUR, "ro be strong;" cp. κύριος, κυρεῖν] *Senate-house.*

custŏdĭ-a, ae, f. (custod-io) *Watch, guard, custody.*

custŏd-ĭo, ĭvi, ītum, īre, a. (custos) *To watch, guard.*

custos, ōdis, com. gen. *A guard, protector.*

D

de, prep. with abl. *From; concerning, on account of.*

dē-bĕo, bŭi, bĭtum, bēre, a. (de; habeo) *To have from : to owe; to be in duty bound to, ought, must.*

dē-cerno, crēvi, crētum, cern-ĕre, a. *To decide, decree.*

dēclĭnā-tĭo, ōnis, f. (declin[a]-o) *A turning aside; a departure; an avoiding, shunning.*

dĕ-dĕcus, ŏris, n. *Disgrace, dishonor.*

dē-fendo, fendi, fensum, fend-ĕre, a *To ward off; to defend, guard.*

dē-fĭcĭo, fēci, fectum, fĭcĕre, a. or n. (de: facio) *To leave; to desert, revolt.*

dē-fīgo, fixi, fixum, fīgĕre, a. *To fix down; to drive: to plunge.*

de-inde, adv. *After this, next, then.*

dēlec-to, tāvi, tātum, tāre, a. intens. (dēlic-io, *to allure*) *To delight, please,*

dēlĕo, ēvi, ētum, ēre, a. *To destroy, annihilate.*

dē-lĭgo, lēgi, lectum, lĭgĕre, a. (de; lego) *To choose out, select.*

dē-migro. migrāvi, migrātum, migrāre, n. *To migrate from; to emigrate; to depart.*

dēnĭque, adv. *At length, finally; in a word, briefly.*

dē-pōno, pŏsŭi, pŏsĭtum, pōnĕre, a. *To lay down; to lay aside.*

dē-prĕcor, prĕcātus sum, prĕcāre, dep. (de ; precor, *to pray*) *To avert by prayer; to avert.*

dē-rĕlĭnquo, līqui, līctum, rĕlinquĕre, a. *To abandon, desert.*

dē-scrībo, scripsi, scriptum, scrĭbĕre, a. *To mark off, to divide.*

dē-sīdĕro, sīdĕrāvi, sīdĕrātum, sīdĕrāre, v. a. *To long for, desire; to miss; to regret, require.*

dē-signo, signāvi, signātum, signāre, v. a. (de ; signo, *to mark*) *To mark out, designate; to elect.*

dē-sĭno, sīvi or sii, sĭtum, sĭnĕre, a. and n. *To leave off, cease.*

dē-sisto, stĭti, stĭtum, n. *To desist.*

dē-sum, esse, fŭi, n. *To be away, to fail, be wanting.*

dē-testor, testātus sum, testāri, dep. (de ; testor, *to be a witness*) *To curse ; to deprecate.*

dētrĭ-mentum, i, n. (for deter-[i]mentum, fr. deter-o, *that which rubs off*) *Loss, damage.*

deus, i, m. *A god.*

dē-ŏvĕo, vōvi, vōtum, vŏvēre, a. *To vow, devote.*

dexter, tĕra, tĕrum, and tra, trum, adj. *Right, on the right ; dextra, ae, f., the right hand.*

dīco, dixi, dictum, dīcĕre, a. [DIC, "to point out"] *To say, assert.*

dĭes, ēi, m. (in sing. sometimes f.) *A day ; in dies, from day to day, daily* (with an idea of increase).

diffĭcul-tas, ātis, f. (for difficil-tas, fr. difficil-is, the state or condition of) *Difficulty, perplexity.*

dignus, a, um, adj. [root DIC, "to point out"] *Worthy.*

dīlĭg-ens, entis, part. (dilig-o) *Careful, diligent.*

dīlĭgen-ter, adv. (diligens) *Attentively, diligently, earnestly.*

dīlĭgent-ĭa, ae, f. (diligens, the quality of the) *Diligence.*

dī-mitto, mīsi, missum, mĭttĕre, a. *To dismiss.*

dīrep-tĭo, ōnis, f. (for dĭrap-tio, fr. dĭrap, true root of dirip-io) *A plundering, pillaging.*

dis-cēdo, cessi, cessum, cēdĕre, n. *To depart.*

dis-cerno, crēvi, crētum, cernĕre, a. *To separate, divide.*

disces-sus, sus, m. (for disced-sus, fr. disced-o, the action of) *A departure.*

discĭpl-īna, ae, f. (for discipul-ina, fr. discipul-us, a thing pertaining to the) *Instruction ; science, skill ; custom, method, discipline.*

dissĭmŭl-o, āvi, ātum, āre, a. (dissimil-is) *To pretend a thing is not what it is ; to dissemble.*

dissŏlū-tus, v, um, part. (for dissolv-tus, fr. dissolv-o) *Lax, remiss, negligent.*

dis-trĭbŭo, tribui, tribūtum, trĭbŭére, a. *To distribute.*

dĭ-u, adv. (di-es) *A long time, long.*

do, dăre, dĕdi, dătum, a. *To give, give up.*

dŏl-or, ōris, m. (dol-eo) *Pain, sorrow.*

dŏmes-tĭcus, a, um, adj. (dom-s) *Domestic, private.*

dŏmus, ūs and i (domi, loc.), f. *A house, abode ; domi, at home.*

dŭb-ĭto, ĭtāvi, ĭtātum, ĭtāre, n. intens. (primitive form du-bo, fr. du-o, *to vibrate to and fro*) *To doubt, hesitate.*

dūco, duxi, ductum, dūcĕre, a. *To lead, conduct.*

dum, conj. *While, as long as, until, if.*

dŭo, ae, o, card. num. adj. *Two.*

dŭodĕcĭm-us, a, um, ord. num. adj. (duodecim) *The twelfth.*

dux, dŭcis, com. gen. (dŭco) *A leader, commander, general.*

E

ē, prep. with abl.; see ex.

ec-quis, quod (ec = e ; quis), inter. subst. pron. *Whether any? any one? any thing?*

ēd-ūco, duxi, ductum, dūcĕre, a. *To lead forth.*

ef-fĕro, ferre, extŭli, ēlātum, a. Irr. (ex ; fero) *To bring forth ; to lift up, exalt.*

effrēnă-tus, a, um, part. (effren[a]-o, *to unbridle*) *Unbridled.*

ef-fŭgĭo, fūgi, no sup., fŭgĕre, (ex; fugio), n. or a. *To flee away ; escape, avoid.*

ĕgo, pers. pron. *I.*

ē-grĕdĭor, gressus sum, grĕdi, dep. (ex ; gradior) *To go out.*

ē-jĭcĭo, jēci, jectum, jĭcĕre, a. (e ; jacio) *To drive out ; to expel, banish.*

ē-lābor, lapsus sum, lābi, dep. *To slip* or *glide away.*

ē-lūdo, lūsi, lūsum, lūdĕre, a. *To delude, deceive, cheat.*

ē-mitto, mīsi, missum, mittĕre, a. *To send forth.*

ē-mŏrĭor, mortuus sum, mŏri, dep. *To die quite ; to perish.*

ĕnim, conj. *For ; etenim, for, you see.*

ĕo, Ire, ĭvi or ĭi, ĭtum, n. *To go.*

ĕōdem, dat. of idem, used adverbially. *To the same place.*

ĕqu-e-s, ĭtis, m. (for equ-i-[t]-s, fr. equ-us) *A horseman ; a horse-soldier ;* in pl., *cavalry ;* equites, the order of *knights.*

ē-rĭpĭo, rĭpŭi, reptum, rĭpĕre, a. (e ; rapio) *To snatch ; to remove, take away.*

ē-rumpo, rūpi, ruptum, rumpĕre, n. *To break out, sally forth.*

et, conj. *And ; et . . . et, both . . . and, not only . . . but also.*

ĕtĕnim : see enim.

ĕtĭam, conj. *And also, besides ; and even, yet, indeed.*

ē-verto, verti, versum, vertĕre, a. *To overthrow ; to subvert, destroy.*

ēvŏcā-tor, ōris, m. (evoc[a]o) *The one who calls forth* (to arms); *summoner.*

ēx or **ē** (e only before consonants). *Out of, from ; immediately after; on account of.*

exaudĭo, audīvi, audītum, audĭre, a. *To hear distinctly.*

ex-cĭdo, cĭdi, no sup., cĭdĕre, n. (ex-cado) *To fall out* or *down ; to slip out.*

ex-clūdo, clūsi, clūsum, clūdĕre, a. (ex ; claudo) *To exclude.*

ex-ĕo, Ire, ĭi, ĭtum, n. *To go forth, depart.*

ex-ercĕo, ŭi, ĭtum, ercēre, a. (ex ; arceo) *To drive on, exercise.*

ex-haurīo, hausi, haustum, haurīre, a. *To draw out; take away; to drain.*

ex-īstīmo, istīmāvi, istīmātum, istīmāre. *To judge, consider.*

exī-tīum, ii, n. (exi, true root of exeo) *Destruction, ruin.*

exsīl-īum, ii, n. (for exsul-ium, fr. exsul, the condition of an) *Banishment, exile.*

ex-sisto, stīti, stītum, sistēre, n. *To step forth; to appear; to be, exist.*

ex-specto, spectāvi, spectātum, spectāre, a. *To await, expect.*

ex-stinguo, stinxi, stinctum, stingēre, a. (ex; stinguo, *to extinguish*) *To put out; extinguish, destroy.*

ex-sul, ūlis, com. gen. (ex; solum; *one who is banished from his native soil*) *An exile.*

ex-sulto, tāvi, tātum, tāre, n. intens. (for ex-salto, fr. exsal, true root of exsil-io) *To leap; exult, rejoice.*

ex-torqueo, torsi, tortum, torquēre, a. *To wrench out, wrest away.*

extrā, adv. and prep. with acc. *Outside of, beyond.*

F

fācīl-e, adv. (facil-is) *Easily, readily.*

fāc-īnus, ōris, n. (fac-io, *the thing done*) *A deed; a bad deed.*

fāc-īo, fēci, factum, fācēre, a.; pass., fīo, fieri, factus sum. *To make, do, perform; to cause.*

falc-ārīus, ii, m. (falx) *A scythe-maker.*

fa'lo, fefelli, falsum, fallēre, a. *To deceive; to escape the notice.*

fal-sus, a, um, part. (for fall-sus, fr. fall-o) *Deceptive; false, untrue.*

fāma, ae, f. *Report, rumour; fame, reputation; infamy, ill-fame.*

fāmes, is, f. *Hunger, famine.*

fā-tĕor, fassus sum, fatēri, dep. a. (f[a]-or) *To confess.*

fauces, ium, f. pl. *The throat; a narrow way, defile.*

fax, fācis, f. *A torch.*

fēbris, is, f. (ferveo, "to burn" *Fever.*

fĕro, ferre, tūli, lātum, a. irreg [roots are FER and TΓL. The second root has the form TOL, TLA, TAL. The supine *latum* = *tlatum* is from this latter root] *To bear, carry; to get receive; to suffer, endure; to say report, relate.*

ferrum, i, n. *Iron, an iron weapon, a sword.*

fīnis, is [for fidnis; root FID, root of findo, "to divide"] m. and f. *A limit, end.*

fīo (pass. of facio), fieri, factus sum. *To be done; to become.*

firm-o, āvi, ātum, āre, a. (firmus) *To make firm; to strengthen.*

firmus, a, um, adj. *Strong.*

flāgīt-īum, ii, n. (flagit-o) *A shameful or disgraceful act; shame*

foed-us, ĕris, n. (for fīdus, fr. fido; *a trusting*) *A league, treaty.*

fōre = futurus esse.

fort-as-se, adv. (for forte; an; sit) *Perhaps.*

fortis, e, adj. *Courageous, brave.*

fort-ītūdo, īnis, f. (fortis) *Firmness, courage, resolution.*

fort-ūna, ae, f. (fors, that which belongs to) *Chance, fortune; in pl., property.*

fŏrum, i, n. [akin to root FER, FOR, "to go through;" cp. πόρος] *The market place; Forum*, which was a long open space between the Capitoline and Palatine Hills, surrounded by porticoes and the shops of bankers; *a market town, mart.*

frango, frēgi, fractum, frangēre, a. [root FRAG, "to break"] *To break; to subdue.*

frĕquent-īa, ae, f. [root FAUC, "to cram"] *An assembly, multitude, concourse.*

frīgus, ōris, n. *Cold.*

frons, frontis, f. *The forehead, brow.*

fŭg-a, ae, f. (fug-io) *Flight.*

fūnes-tus, a, um, adj. (for funertus; fr. funus, *death*) *Causing death; fatal, destructive.*

fŭrĭ-ōsus, a, um, adj. (furi-ae) *Full of madness; raging, furious.*

fŭr-or, ōris, m. (fur-o) *A raging, madness.*

G

gaudĭum, ĭi, n. (gaudeo) *Gladness, delight, pleasure.*

gĕl-ĭdus, a, um, adj. (gel-o, *to freeze*) *Icy cold.*

gen-s, tis, f. (gen-o=gigno, *to beget; that which is begotten*) *A clan; a tribe, nation.*

glădĭ-ātor, ōris, m. (gladi-us, *one using a*) *A swordsman; a gladiator.*

glădĭus, ĭi, m. *A sword.*

glōr-ĭa, ae, f. (akin to clarus) *Glory.*

grăd-us, ūs, m. (grad-ior, *to walk*) *A step; a degree.*

grāt ĭa, ae, f. (grat-us, the quality of the) *Regard, love; gratitude; thanks.*

grăvis, e, adj. *Heavy; severe; grave, impressive; venerable.*

grăv-ĭter, adv. *Violently, severely.*

H

hăbĕo, ŭi, ĭtum, hăbēre, a. *To have, hold; to do, perform, make; to give.*

hăb-ĭto, ĭtāvi, ĭtātum, ĭtāre, intens., a. and n. (hab-eo) *To inhabit; live; to stay.*

haereo, haesi, haesum, haerēre, n. *To stick, adhere.*

hebe-sco, no perf., no sup., scēre, n. inch. (hebe-o, *to be blunt*) *To be dull.*

hīc, haec, hoc, pron. demonstr. *This.*

hīc-ce, intensive form of hic.

hīc, adv. *Here.*

hŏmo, ĭnis, com. gen. *A human being; man or woman; person.*

hŏnest-o, āvi, ātum, āre, a. *To adorn; to honor.*

hŏnes-tus, a, um, adj. (for honor-tus, fr. honor) *Regarded with honor; honored, noble.*

hŏnor (os), ōris. m. *Honor; official dignity, office.*

hōra, ae, f. *An hour.*

horr-ĭbĭlis, e, adj. (horr-eo, *to be trembled at*) *Terrible, fearful, horrible.*

hortor, ātus sum, āre, dep. *To strongly urge, exhort.*

hostis, is, com. gen. *An enemy.*

hŭmus, i, f. *The ground;* humi (loc.), *on the ground.*

I

ĭdem, eadem, idem, pron. (root i, suffix dem) *The same.*

ĭdūs, uum, f. pl. *The Ides.*

ĭgĭtur, conj. *Then; therefore, accordingly; well then.*

i-gnōmin-ĭa, ae, f. (for in-gnomin-ia; fr. in, gnomen = nomen, *a depriving of one's good name*) *Disgrace, ignominy.*

i-gnō-ro, a. (for in-gno-ro; fr. in, not; gno, root of gnosco = nosco) *Not to know, to be ignorant of.*

ille, a, ud, pron. demonstr. *That; he, she, it.*

illĕc-ĕbra, ae, f. (for illac-ebra, fr. illac, true root of illic-o, *to allure*) *An enticement, allurement.*

illust-ro, a. [in, LUC, "to shine:" cp. lux] *To light up, illumine; to make clear.*

immān-ĭtas, ātis, f. (immanis, *huge*) *Hugeness, enormity.*

im-minĕo, no perf., no sup., minēre, n. (in, mineo, *to hang over*) *To border upon, be near, impend.*

im-mitto, mīsi, missum, mittēre, a. (in; mitto) *To send into; to let loose.*

immo, adv. (etym. dub.) *On the under side, on the reverse; on the contrary; no indeed, by no means; yes indeed.*

im-mortālis, e, adj. (in; mortalis, *mortal*) *Immortal.*

impĕd-ĭo, ĭvi, ĭtum, ĭre, a. (in; pes, *to get the feet in something*) *To hinder, prevent.*

im-pendĕo, no perf., no sup., pendēre, n. (in; pendeo, *to hang*) *To hang over; to impend, threaten.*

impĕrā-tor, ōris, m. (imper-[a]-o) *A general; chief.*

im-pĕritus, a, um, adj. (in; perĭtus, *skilled*) *Inexperienced, ignorant.*

impĕr-ĭum, ĭ, n. (imper-o) *Authority, power, empire, government.*

im-pĕro, pĕrāvĭ, pĕrātum, pĕrāre, a. (in; patro, *to bring to pass*) *To accomplish; obtain.*

impĕtus, ūs, m. (impeto, *to attack*) *An attack.*

im-pĭus, a, um, adj. (in; pius, *pious*) *Not pious, irreverent, unpatriotic.*

im-portū-nus, a, um, adj. (for in-portu-nus, fr. in; portus) *Unsuitable; savage; dangerous.*

im-prŏbus, a, um, adj. (in; probus) *Wicked, base.*

im-pūnitus, a, um, adj. (in; punitus, *punished*) *Not punished; unpunished.*

in, prep. with acc. and abl. *In, into, against; of time, up to, for, into, through;* with ablative, *in, upon, on.*

ĭnānis, e, adj. *Empty, void.*

incend-ĭum, ĭi, n. (incend-o) *A burning, conflagration, fire.*

in-clūdo, clūsi, clūsum, clūdĕre, a. *To shut up; to include.*

in-crēdĭbilis, e, adj. *Incredible, extraordinary.*

increpo, (āvi) ui, (ātum) ĭtum, āre, n. and a. *To make a noise.*

in-dūco, duxi, ductum, dūcĕre, a. *To introduce; to lead into, persuade.*

in-ĕo, ĭre, ĭi, ĭtum, n. or a. *To go into, enter; begin.*

inert-ĭa, ae, f. (inners, the quality of the) *Want of skill; inactivity.*

in-fĕro, ferre, intŭli, illātum, a. irr. *To produce, make; to bring, put, or place upon.*

infestus, a, um, adj. *Hostile, dangerous.*

infĭti-or, dep. (infĭti-ae, *denial*) *To deny.*

in-flammo, flammāvĭ, flammātum, flammāre, a. *To set on fire.*

in-grăvesco, no perf., no sup., grăvescĕre, n. *To grow heavy; to grow worse.*

ĭn-ĭmĭcus, a, um, adj. (in; amicus) *Unfriendly;* as noun, m., *a private enemy.*

ĭnĭtĭ-o, a. (initi-um) *To begin, to initiate, consecrate.*

injūrĭ-a, ae, f. (injuri-us, *injurious*) *Injury, wrong;* injuriā, as adv., *unjustly.*

inl : see ill.

ĭnŏp-ĭa, ae, f. (inops) *Need.*

inquam, def. verb- *To say.*

inr : see irr.

inscrībo, scripsi, scriptum, scrībĕre, a. *To write upon; to inscribe; to impress upon.*

insĭd-ĭae, ārum, f. pl. (insid-eo, *to sit in*) *An ambush, ambuscade; plot treachery.*

insĭdĭ-or, atus sum, ari, dep. (insidiae) *To wait for, expect; to plot against.*

intel-lego, lexi, lectum, lĕgĕre, a. (inter : lego, *to choose between*) *To perceive, understand.*

in-tendo, tendi, tentum, tendĕre, and tensum, a. *To stretch out; to strive; to aim at.*

inter, prep. with acc. *Between, among.*

inter-cēdo, cessi, cessum, cēdĕre, n. *To go or come between; to intervene.*

inter-fĭcĭo, fēci, fectum, fĭcĕre, a. (inter; facio) *To destroy; to kill.*

intĕrĭ-tus, ūs, m. (intereo) *Destruction; death.*

inter-rŏgo, rŏgāvi, rŏgātum, rŏgāre, a. *To ask, inquire.*

inter-sum, esse, fui, n. irr. *To be between; to differ;* interest, impers., *it interests.*

intes-tīnus, a, um, adj. (for intus-tinus, fr. intus) *Internal; intestine, civil.*

intrā, prep. with acc. *Within, in.*

in-ūro, ussi, ustum, ūrĕre, a. *To burn into; to brand.*

in-vĕnĭo, vēni, ventum, vĕnīre, a. *To come upon, find.*

invĭd-ĭa, ae, f. (invid-us, *an envier*) *Envy, jealousy, unpopularity.*

invīto, āvi, ātum, āre, a. *To ask, invite, summon.*

i-pse, a, um, pron. demonstr. (for i -pse; fr. is and suffix pse) *Himself, herself, itself; he, she, it; very.*

ir-rētĭ-o, vi, ĭtum, īre, a. (for in-ret-io, fr. in; ret-e, *a net) To ensnare, captivate.*

is, ea, id. pron. demonstr. *This, that; he, she, it; such.*

is-te, ta, tud, pron. demonstr. (is; suffix te) *This of yours; this, that; that fellow, that thing* (used with contempt).

ĭta, adv. *In this way; so, thus.*

J

jăcĕo, ui, jacĭtum, ēre, n. *To lie; to lie down.*

jac-to, tāvi, tātum, tāre, a. freq. (jac-io) *To throw; to toss about; to boast, vaunt.*

jam, adv. *Now, already;* jam-dūdum, *a long time since, long ago* (with a present tense, giving the force of the perfect brought down to the present time); jam-prīdem, adv. *long time ago, for a long time.*

jŭbĕo, jussi, jussum, jŭbēre, a. *To command, order, bid.*

jŭ-cundus, a, um, adj. (for juv-cundus, fr. juv-o) *Pleasant, agreeable, pleasing.*

jūdĭc-ĭum, ii, n. (judic-o) *A judging; a judgment; a sentence.*

jŭ-dico, āvi, ātum, āre, a. (jus; dico) *To judge; to think.*

jungo, junxi, junctum, jungĕre, a. *To join, unite.*

jŭ-s, jūris, n. (akin to root ju, *to join) Law, right, justice;* jure, *justly.*

jus-sŭ, m. (only in abl sing.; jubeo) *By command.*

jus-tus, a, um, adj. (for jur-tus, fr. jus) *Just, right.*

L

lăbefac-to, tāvi, tātum, tāre, a. intens. (labefac-o) *To cause to totter; to injure, ruin; to imperil.*

lăbor, ōris, m. *Labor, toil.*

laet-ĭtĭa, ae, f. (laet-us) *Joy, gladness.*

lātro, (a short or long), ōnis, m. *A robber, highwayman.*

latrŏcīn-ĭum, ii, n. (latro) *Highway robbery, plundering.*

laus, laudis, f. *Praise, fame, honor.*

lectŭ-lus, i, m. dim. (for lectolus, fr. lecto, stem of lectus) *A little couch, bed.*

lēnis, e, adj. *Soft, gentle, mild.*

lex, lēgis, f. (= leg-s, fr. lĕg-o; *that which is read) A law.*

līber, ĕra, ĕrum, adj. *Free, unrestrained.*

lībĕr-i, ōrum, m. pl. (liber) *Children.*

lībĕr-o, āvi, ātum, āre, a. (id.) *To make free; to free.*

lib-īdo, ĭnis, f. (lib-et) *Desire; passion, lust.*

līcet, uit, itum est, ēre, imp. *It is permitted; one may or can.*

lŏcus, i, m. *A place* (in pl., loci or loca).

long-e, adv. (long-us) *Far off; greatly, much; by far.*

lŏquor, lŏcūtus sum, lŏqui, dep. *To speak, say.*

lux, lūcis, f. (=luc-s, fr. luc-eo, *to shine) Light; the light of day, daylight.*

M

māchĭn-or, ātus sum, āri, dep. (machin-a, *a device) To contrive, devise; to plot.*

mac-to, tāvi, tātum, tāre, a. intens. (for mag-to, fr. obsolete mag-o, of same root as found in mag-nus) *To venerate, honor; to kill, slay; to immolate; to destroy.*

mă-gis, adv. *More.*

mag-nus, a, um, adj. (comp. major, sup. maximus; root mag) *Great;* majores, *ancestors.*

māj-or, us, adj. comp. (magnus)

mallĕŏ-lus, i, m. dim. (malleus, *a hammer) A small hammer; a kind of fire-dart.*

mā-lo, malle, mālŭi, a. irr. (contracted fr. mag-volo, fr. root mag;

volo, *to have a great desire for*) To prefer.

măl-um, i, n. (malus) *An evil.*

man-do. dăvi, dătum, dăre, a. (man-us; do, *to put into one's hand*) *To order; to commend, consign, intrust; to lay up; se fugae mandare, to take to flight.*

mănus, ūs, f. *A hand; band of troops.*

mărit-us, a, um, adj. (marit-a, mas) *Matrimonial, conjugal; as noun, m. (sc. vir), a husband.*

mătūr-ē, adv. (matur-us) *Seasonably, at the proper time; soon.*

mătūr-ĭtas, ātis, f. (matur-us) *Ripeness, maturity, perfection.*

maxĭm-ē, adv. (maxim-us) *In the highest degree, especially.*

mědĭocr-ĭter, adv. (mediocr:is) *Moderately.*

mědĭtor, ātus sum, āri, dep. *To think, consider, meditate upon; to practise.*

mehercŭle, mehercle, mehercules, adv. *By Hercules.*

měmĭni, isse, a. and n., dep. *To remember, recollect.*

měmōrĭa, ae, f. (memor, mindful) *Memory.*

mens, mentis, f. *The mind; thought, purpose.*

mětŭ-o, ŭi, ūtum, a. and n. (metu-s) *To fear.*

mětus, ūs, m. *Fear.*

mě us, a, um, pron. pers. (me) *My, mine.*

mĭn-us, adv. (min-or) *Less, not.*

mĭsĕrĭcord-ĭā, ae, f. (misericors, pitiful) *Pity, compassion.*

mitto, mīsi, missum, mittĕre, a. *To let go, send.*

mŏdo, adv. *Only; non modo... sed etiam, not only; ... but also.*

mŏdus, i, m. *A measure; limit; manner; kind.*

moenĭa, ium, n. pl. *Defensive walls; ramparts; city walls.*

mōles, is, f. *A huge mass; greatness, might.*

mŏl-ĭor, ĭtus sum, īri, dep., n. and a. (mol-es) *To endeavor, strive; to undertake; to plot; to prepare.*

mol-lis, e, adj. (for mov-lis, fr. mov-eo, *that may or can be moved*) *Weak, feeble; gentle; mild.*

mŏra, ae, f. *A delay.*

morbus, i, m. *A sickness, disease.*

mor-s, tis, f. (mor-ior) *Death.*

mor tŭus, a, um, part. (mor-ior) *Dead.*

mos, mōris, m. [for meors; from meo, are, "to go"] *Usage, custom, practice.*

mŏvĕo, mōvi, mōtum, mŏvēre, a. *To move; to affect.*

mult-ō, adv. (mult-us) *Much, greatly.*

mult-o (mulcto), āvi, ātum, āre (mult-a, *a fine*) *To fine; to punish.*

multus, a, um, adj. *Much; in pl., many.*

mūn-ĭo, īvi, ĭtum, īre, a: (moenia) *To fortify.*

mūni-tus, a, um, part. (muni-o) *Fortified, secure.*

mūrus, i, m. [for mun-rus; root MUN, "to defend"] *A wall.*

mū-to, tāvi, tātum, tāre, a. intens. (for mov-to, fr. mov-eo) *To move; to alter, change.*

N

nam, conj. *For.*

nanciscor, nanctus and nactus sum, nancisci, dep. *To get; to find.*

nascor, nātus sum, nasci, dep. *To be born; to spring forth; to grow.*

nā-tūra, ae, f. (na-scor; *a being born*) *Birth; nature.*

nau-frăgus, a, um, adj. (nav-frag-us; navis; frag, root of frango) *That suffers shipwreck; wrecked.*

ně, adv. and conj. *No, not; ne ... quidem, not even; that not, lest.*

-ně, interrog. and enclitic particle, in direct questions with the ind. asking merely for information; in indirect questions with the subj. *Whether.*

nec, conj.: see neque.

něcess-ărĭus, a, um, adj. (necess-e) *Unavoidable, necessary; as noun, m., a relative, friend.*

nĕ-ces-se, neut. adj. (found only in nom. and acc. sing., for ne-ced-se, fr. ne; ed-o, *not yielding*) *Unavoidable, necessary.*

nĕfār-ĭus, a. um, adj. (for nefasius, fr. nefas) *Impious, nefarious.*

nĕg-lĕgo, lexi, lectum, lĕgĕre, a. (nec; lego, *not to gather*) *To neglect, disregard.*

nĕgo, nĕgāvi, nĕgātum, nĕgāre, n. and a. *To say "no;" to deny.*

nĕ-mo, ĭnis, m. and f. (ne; homo) *No person, no one, nobody.*

nĕ-que or nec, adv. *Not;* conj., *and not;* neque . . . neque, nec, . . . nec, *neither* . . , *nor.*

nēqu-ĭtĭa, ae, f. nequ-am) *Badness; inactivity, negligence.*

ne-scĭo, scīvi, scītum, scīre, a. *Not to know, to be ignorant of.*

nex, nĕcis, f. (= nec-s, fr. nec-o) *Death; murder, slaughter.*

nĭhil, n. indecl. (nihilum, by apocope) *Nothing; not at all.*

nĭmis, adv. *Too much; too.*

nĭmĭ-um, adv. (nimi-us) *Too much; too.*

nĭ-si, conj. *If not, unless.*

noct-urnus, a, um, adj. (nox) *Belonging to the night, nocturnal.*

nōmĭn-o (1), a. (nomen) *To name.*

nōn, adv. *Not, no.*

non-dum, adv. *Not yet.*

non-ne, inter. adv. (expects answer "yes") *Not?*

non-nullus, a, um, adj. (not one) *Some, several.*

nost r, tra, trum, poss. pron. (nos) (*ur, our own, ours;* in plur., as noun, m., *our men.*

nōta, ae, f. (nosco) *A mark, sign; a brand.*

nŏt-o, tāvi, tātum, tāre, a. (not-a) *To mark, designate.*

nŏvus, a, um, adj. *New.*

nox, noctis, f. *Night.*

nūdus, a, um, adj. *Naked, bare.*

n-ullus, a, um, adj. (ne; ullus) *None, no.*

num, inter. particle, used in direct questions expecting the answer "no;" in indirect questions, *Whether.*

nŭmĕrus, i, m. *A number.*

nunc, adv. *Now, at present.*

n-unquam (nunquam), adv. (ne; unquam) *Never.*

nūper, adv. (for nov-per, fr. novus) *Newly, lately.*

nupt-ĭae, ārum, f. pl. (nupt-a, *a married woman*) *Marriage, nuptials.*

O

O, interj. *O! Oh!*

ob, prep. with acc. *On account of.*

ŏbĕo, ire, ĭi, ĭtum, n. *To engage in, execute.*

oblīviscor, oblītus sum, oblivisci, dep. *To forget.*

obscūr-ē, adv. (obscur-us) *Indistinctly, secretly.*

obscūr-o, āvi, ātum, āre, a. (obscurus) *To obscure.*

ŏbscūrus, a, um, adj. *Dark; unknown.*

ob-sĭdĕo, sēdi, sessum, sĭdēre, a. (ob; sedeo, *to sit*) *To sit down at or before; to invest; to watch for.*

ob-sīdo, no perf., no sup., sīdere, a. *To sit down over or against; to invest, besiege.*

ob-sisto, stĭti, stĭtum, sistēre, n. *To oppose, resist.*

ob-sto, stĭti, stātum, stāre, n. *To oppose.*

ob-tempĕro, āvi, ātum, āre, n. *To comply with, obey.*

oc-cīdo, cīdi, cīsum, cīdēre, a. (ob; caedo, *to strike against*) *To strike down; to kill.*

oc-cŭp-o, āvi, ātum, āre, a. (for ob-cap-o, fr. ob; capio) *To take, seize; to occupy.*

ŏcŭlus, i, m. *An eye.*

ŏdi, odisse, a., defective. *To hate.*

ŏd-ĭum, ii, n. (odi) *Hatred.*

of-fendo, fendi, fensum, fendēre, a. *To hit; to offend.*

of-fensus, a, um, adj. *Odious.*

ōmen, ĭnis, n. *An omen.*

o-mitto, mlsi, missum, mittĕre, a. (ob; mitto) *To let go; to pass over, omit.*

omnis, e, adj. *Every, all.*

ŏpīn-or, ātus sum, āri, dep. (opin-us, *thinking*) *To think, suppose, imagine.*

ŏport-et, ūit, ēre, impers. *It is necessary.*

op-prīmo, pressi, pressum, prĭmĕre, a. (ob; premo) *To overwhelm, subdue, overpower; to cover.*

optĭm-as, ātis, adj. (optim-us) *Aristocratic;* as noun (sc. homo), *an aristocrat.*

opt-ĭmus, a, um, adj. (super. of bonus) *Best, very good.*

orbis, is, m. *A circle; the world, the universe.*

ord-o, Inis, m. (ord-ior, *to begin*) *Order; class, degree.*

ōs, ōris, n. *The mouth; the face, countenance.*

osten-to, tāvi, tātum, tāre, a. intens. (for ostend-to, fr. ostendɪo) *To show; to display.*

ōtĭ-ōsus, a, um, adj. (oti-um, full of) *At leisure; quiet; calm, tranquil.*

ōtĭum, ii, n. *Leisure.*

P

pa-ciscor, pactus sum, pacisci, dep., n. and a. *To contract; to agree, bargain.*

pac-tum, i, n. (pac-iscor) *An agreement, compact; manner, way.*

pango, pangĕre, panxi, pactum. *To agree.*

par-ens, entis, m. and f. (par-io) *A parent.*

părĭes, ietis, m. *A wall.*

părĭo, pĕpĕri, părĭtum, părĕre and partum, a. *To bring forth; to obtain.*

păr-o, āvi, ātum, āre, a. *To make, get ready, prepare.*

parrĭ-cida, ae, m. (for patr-i-caed-a, fr. pater; [i]; caedo) *The murderer of one's father; parricide.*

parricīd-ium, ii, n. (parricid-a) *Parricide, murder, treason.*

pars, partis, f. *A part, portion.*

part-ĭ-cep-s, cĭpis, adj. (for part-i-cap-s, fr. pars; [i]; cap-io) *Sharing, partaking;* as noun, *a sharer, partaker.*

parvus, a, um, adj. *Small, little, slight.*

pat-e-făcĭo, fēci, factum, făcĕre, a. (pateo; facio) *To disclose, expose, bring to light.*

pătĕo, ŭi, no sup., pătĕre, n. *To stand or lie open; to be clear, plain.*

păter, tris, m. *A father.*

pătĭent-ĭa, ae, f. (patior) *Patience.*

pătr-ĭus, a, um (a long or short), adj. (pater) *Paternal, fatherly;* as noun, f. (sc. te ra), *native land, country.*

paucus, a, um, adj. *Small, little;* as noun, pl. m., *few, a few.*

paul-isper, adv. (paul-us, *little*) *For a little while.*

paul-ō, adv. (id., *little*) *By a little, a little.*

paul-um, adv. (paul-us) *By a little, a little.*

paul-us, a, um, adj. *A little, small.*

pĕnĭ-tus, adv. (root pen) *From within; deeply.*

per, prep. with acc. *Through; by, by means of; on account of.*

per-cĭpĭ-o, cēpi, ceptum, cĭpĕre, a. (per; capio) *To take possession of, seize; to comprehend, perceive, learn.*

perd-ĭtus, a, um, part. (perd-o) *Ruined, desperate, abandoned.*

per-do, dĭdi, dĭtum, dĕre, a. *To destroy, ruin.*

per-fĕro, ferre, tŭli, lātum, a. irr. *To bear, endure.*

per-fringo, frēgi, fractum, fringĕre, a. (per; frango) *To break through; to violate, infringe.*

per-frŭor, fructus sum, frŭi, dep. *To enjoy fully.*

per-go, perrexi, perrectum, pergĕre, a. and n. (for per-rego, *to make quite straight*) *To proceed, go on.*

pĕrĭcl-ĭtor, ĭtātus sum, tari, dep., a. and n. (pericl-um) *To try; to endanger, risk; to venture, hazard.*

pĕrĭ-cŭlum (clum), i, n. (perl-or [obsolete], to go through) A trial; hazard, danger, peril.

per-mitto, mĭsi, missum, mit-tĕre, a. To send through; to give up, intrust, surrender.

per-mŏvĕo, mōvi, mōtum, mŏ-vēre, a. To move thoroughly; to excite, arouse.

pernĭc-ĭes, ĭēi, f. (pernec-o, to kill utterly) Destruction.

pernĭcĭ-ōsus, a, um, adj. (per-nici-es, full of) Very destructive, ruinous, pernicious.

perpĕtŭus, a, um, adj. Con-tinuous; constant, perpetual.

per-saepe. Very often, very frequently.

per-spĭcĭo, spexi, spectum, spĭ-cĕre, a. (per; specio, to look) To look through; to perceive, note.

per-terrĕo, ŭi, ĭtum, terrēre, a. To terrify thoroughly.

per-tĭme-sco, timŭi, no sup. timescĕre, a. and n. inch. (pertimeo To fear or dread greatly.

per-tĭnĕō, tĭnŭi, tentum, tĭnĕre, n. (per; teneo) To stretch; to con-cern; to pertain to.

per-vĕnĭo, vēni, ventum, vĕnĭre, n. To arrive at, reach.

pestis. is, f. Ruin, plague.

pĕt-ĭtĭo, ōnis, f. (pet-o) An at-tack, thrust.

pĕto, pĕtīvi, pĕtītum, pĕtĕre, a. To seek; to attack, thrust at.

plăcĕo, ŭi, ĭtum, plăcēre, n. To please; placet, impers., it seems good; it is resolved upon; it is de-termined.

plăco, āvi, ātum, āre, a. To quiet, calm, reconcile.

plăn-ē, adv. (plan-us) Simply, clearly.

plēbes, ei, f. or plebs, plēbis, f. The common people, the plebeians.

plŭ-rĭmus, a, um, sup. adj. (multus) Very much; in pl., the largest or smaller number; with quam, as many as possible.

poena, ae, f. Punishment.

pol-lĭcĕor, licitus sum, lĭcēri, dep. (pot, root of pot-is, powerful, and liceor, to bid) To promise.

pontĭfex. ficis, m. The high priest, pontiff.

pŏpŭlus, i, m. A people, nation, multitude.

porta, ae, f. A gate; passage.

pos-sum, posse, pŏtŭi, no sup., n. irr. (for pot-sum, fr. pot, root of pot-is, able, and sum) To be able.

post, adv. and prep. with acc. Behind; after; next to, since.

post-ĕā, adv. After this; after-wards.

postĕr-ĭtas, ātis, f. (poster-us) Futurity; posterity.

postŭlo, a. To ask, demand, request.

pŏtĭus, adv. (adv. neut. of potior, comp. of potis) Rather, more.

prae-clārus, a, um, adj. Splen-did, excellent; distinguished.

prae-dĭco, dĭcāvi, dĭcātum, dĭ-cāre, a. To publish, state. declare.

prae-dĭco, dixi, dictum, dĭcĕre, a. To say beforehand; to predict.

prae-fĕro, ferre, tŭli, lātum, a. irr. To bear before; to display, to exhibit.

prae-mitto, mĭsi, missum, mit-tĕre, a. To send forward.

prae-s-ens, entis, adj. (prae; sum) Present.

praesent-ĭa, ae, f. (praesens) Presence.

praesĭd-ĭum, ii, n. (praesid-eo) A guarding, defence, aid; a garri-son, guard.

prae-stōlor (1), dep. n. and a. To wait for.

praetĕr-ĕo, ĭre, ii, ĭtum, n. and a. irr. To pass over, omit.

praeter-mitto, mĭsi, missum, mittĕre, a. To pass over, omit.

prae-tor, ōris, m. (for praei-tor; fr. praeeo) A leader; a praetor, an officer next to consul in rank.

prĭ-dem, adv. (for prae-dem, fr. prae; suffix dem) A long time ago, long since.

prĭ-dĭē, adv. (for prae-die, fr. prae; dies) On the day before.

prĭ-mŏ, adv. (primus) At first.

pri-mus, a, um, sup. adj. (for prae-mus, fr. prae, with superlative suffix mus) *The first, first.*

prin-cep-s, cĭpis, adj. (for prim-caps, fr. prim-us; cap-io) *First*; as noun, m. and f., *chief, leader.*

pri-or, us, gen. ōrĭs, comp. adj. (for -prae-or, fr. prae; comparative suffix or) *Former.*

privā-tus, a, um, part. (prĭv-[a]-o, *to deprive*) *Private*; as noun, m., *a private citizen.*

prob-o, āvi, ātum, āre, a. *To try; to approve.*

perfec-tĭo, ōnis, f. (for profac-tio, fr. profic-iscor) *A setting out, departure.*

prō-fĭcĭo, fēci, fectum, fĭcĕre, n. and a. (pro; facio) *To accomplish, effect.*

pro-fĭc-ĭscor, fectus sum, fĭcis-cĭ, dep. n. inch. (for pro-fac-iscor, fr. pro; fac-io) *To set out.*

prō-fŭgĭo, fūgi, fŭgitum, fŭgĕre, a. and n. *To flee.*

prŏpe, adv. and prep. with acc. *Nearly, almost.*

prŏprĭus, a, um, adj. *One's one; proper, peculiar, suited to.*

prop-ter, prep. with acc. (prop-e) *Near; on account of.*

pro-sĕquor, sĕcūtus sum, sĕqui, dep. *To follow, accompany.*

proxĭmus, a, um, adj. (proc-si-mus, for prop-simus, fr. prop-e, and sup. ending simus) *The nearest, next; the last.*

publĭc-ē, adv. (public-us) *In behalf of the state, in the name of the state.*

publ-ĭcus, a, um, adj. (populus) *public, common.*

pŭd-or, ōrĭs, m. (pudet) *Shame, modesty.*

pur-go, a. (pūr-us) *To clean, cleanse; purify.*

pŭt-o, āvi, ātum, āre, a. (put-us, *cleansed*) *To make clean; to reckon, think.*

Q

quaero (quaeso), quaesīvi, ii, quaesītum, quaerĕre, a. *To seek; demand, ask.*

quaeso: see quaero.

quaēs-tĭo, ōnis, f. (quaes-o) *A seeking; a judicial investigation.*

quam, adv. (adverbial acc. of quis) *In what manner, how; as much, as; than;* with superlatives, *as (much as) possible,* e.g. quam primum, *as soon as possible.*

quam-dĭu, adv. *How long, as long as.*

quam-ob-rem, rel. adv. *On which account, wherefore.*

quam-quam, conj. *Although.*

quantus, a, um, adj. *How great, how much.*

quā-rē, adv. (quis; res) *From what cause? wherefore?*

-que, enclitic conj. *And;* que . . . que, *both . . . and.*

quĕr-ĭmōnĭa, ae, f. (queror) *A complaint.*

quĕror, questus sum, quĕri, dep. a. and n. *To complain of, lament, bewail.*

qui, quae, quod, rel. pron. *Who, which, what, that.*

qui-dam, quaedam, quoddam, indef. pron. *Some, some one, a certain one.*

quĭdem, adv. *Indeed, at least;* ne . . . quidem, *not even.*

quĭe-sco, quĭēvi, quĭētum, quies-cĕre, n. inch. (for quiet-sco, fr. quies) *To keep quiet.*

quin-tus, a, um, ord. num. adj. (quinqu-tus, fr. quinque) *The fifth.*

quis, quae, quid, interrog. pron. (quis, quae, quod, used adjectively) *Who? which? what?* quid, *how? why? wherefore?* preceded by ne, si, nisl, num, becomes an indefinite pron., *any, some.*

quis-quam, quae-quam, quic-quam (quod-quam), indef. pron. *Any, any one.*

quis-que, quae-que, quod-que (and as noun, quic-que; quid-que), indef. pron. *Each, every,*

quis-quis, quod-quod or quic-quid or quid-quid, indef. pron. *Whatever, whatsoever;* as noun, *whoever, whosoever.*

quō, adv. (qui) *Where; whither.*

quod, conj. (acc. neut. fr. qui) *That, in that, because; quod si, but if.*

quon-dam, adv. (for quom-dam, fr. quom, old form of quem) *Once, formerly.*

quŏn-ïam, conj. (for quom-iam, fr. quom = cum and jam) *Since.*

quŏque, conj. *Also, too* (placed after the word it emphasizes).

quot, num. adj. indecl. *How many, as many.*

quŏtïd-ïe, cotidie. *Daily.*

quot-ïes, iens, adv. (xuot) *How often.*

quŏtïes-cumque, adv. *How often soever; as often as.*

quo-usque, adv. (for quom; us-que, fr. quom, old form of quem; usque) *Until what time; how long.*

R

răpïo, ŭi, raptum, răpĕre, a. *To ma'ch or draw away.*

ră-tïo, ōnis, f. (reor) *A calcula-tion; judgment, reason; course, manner.*

rĕcens, ntis, adj. *Fresh, recent.*

rĕ-cïpïo, cĕpi, ceptum, rĕcïpĕre, a. (re; capio) *To take back; to accept, receive.*

rĕ-cognosco, cognōvi, cogni-tum, cognoscĕre. a. *To know again, recognize; to examine, review.*

rĕ-condo, condïdi, condïtum, condĕre, a. *To put back again; to sheath* (of a sword); *to lay up; bury.*

rec-tus, a, um, part. (for reg-tus, fr. reg-o) *Right; straight.*

red-und-o, āvi, ātum, āre, n. *To overflow; to abound.*

re-fĕro, ferre, tŭli, lātum, a. irr. *To carry, bring,* or *give back; to re-turn, pay back.*

rēgï-ē, adv. (regi-us) *Royally, tyrannically.*

rĕ-lēvo, lĕvāvi, lĕvātum, lĕvāre, a. *To make light; to relieve.*

rĕ-linquo, lïqui, lictum, liu-qŭĕre, a. (re; linquo, *to leave*) *To leave behind, leave.*

rēlïqu-us, a, um, adj. (rel n|qu-o) *Remaining; the remain-der of, rest.*

rĕmănĕo, mansi, no sup., mān-ĕre, n. *To remain behind.*

rĕ-mŏror, mŏrātus sum, mŏrāri, dep., n. and a. *To stay, delay, to detain.*

re-pello, pŭli, pulsum, a. *To reject, repel,*

rĕ-pĕrïo, rĕpĕri, répertum, pĕr-ïre, a. (re; par-o) *To find.*

re-primo, pressi, pressum, a. (re; premo) *To check, restrain.*

rĕpŭdï-o, āvi, ātum, āre, a. (repudi-um, *a casting off*) *To cast off; to reject.*

rēs, rĕi, f. *A thing, matter; res publica, the commonwealth, the state.*

rĕ-sïdĕo, sĕdi, no sup., sïdĕre, n. (re; sedeo) *To remain; to remain behind.*

rĕ-spondĕo, spondi, sponsum, spondĕre, a. (re; spondeo, *to pro-mise*) *To answer, reply.*

respon-sum, i, n. (for respond-sum, fr. respond-eo) *An answer, reply.*

rēs-publïcā, rĕi-publïcae, f. : see res.

rĕ-vŏco, a. *To call back; to recall.*

rŏgo, āvi, ātum, āre, a. *To ask; rogare legem, to propose a law.*

rŭ-ïna, ae, f. (ru-o) *A falling; ruin.*

S

sacr-ārïum, ii (a long or short), n. (sacr-um) *A place for keeping holy things; a shrine.*

sacrum, i (a long or short), n. (sacer) *A sacred thing; a religious rite, ceremony.*

saep-e, adv. (saep-is, *frequent*) *Often, frequently.*

săg-ax, ācis, adj. (sagio, *to per-ceive quickly*) *Sagacious, keen-scented.*

sălŭ-s, ūtis, f. (for salvit-s; fr. salv-eo, *to be well*) *Health; safety, prosperity.*

sălŭt-o, āvi, ātum, āre, a. (salus) *To greet, salute.*

sanc-tus, a, um, adj. (sancio) *Sacred, holy, venerable.*

sanguis, ĭnis, m. *Blood.*

sătelles, ĭtis, com. gen. *An attendant ; an accomplice, partner.*

sătĭs (sat), adv. *Enough.*

sătis-făcĭo, fēci, factum, făcěre, n. *To give satisfaction ; satisfy, content.*

scělěrāt-ē, adv. (scelerat-us) *Impiously, wickedly.*

scělěra-tus, a, um, part. (sceler[a]-o, *to pollute*) *Polluted, bad ; as noun, m., a wretch.*

scělus, ěris, n. *An evil deed ; a crime, guilt.*

scĭo, scĭvi, scĭtum, scīre, a. *To know, perceive.*

sē-cēdo, cessi, cessum, cēděre, n. *To go apart ; to go away.*

sē-cerno, crēvi, crētum, cerněre, a. *To put apart, separate.*

sed, conj. *But, yet, but also ;* non solum . . . sed etiam, *not only . . . but also.*

sēd-ĭ-tĭo, ōnis, f. (sed = sine ; i, root of eo, *a going apart*) *Sedition, strife.*

sē-jungo, junxi, junctum, jungěre, a. *To disjoin ; to separate.*

sē-men, ĭnis, n. (for să-men, fr. sa, true root of sero ; *the sown thing. Seed.*

semper, adv. *Ever, always.*

sěn-ātus, ūs, m. (senex) *The council of the elders, the senate.*

sěnātūs-consultum, i, n. *A decree of the senate.*

sen-sus, ūs, m. (for sent-sus, fr. sent-io) *Perception, feeling.*

sentent-ĭa, ae, f. (for sentient-ia, fr. sentiens, *thinking*) *An opinion, sentiment ; sentence, vote.*

sentīna, ae, f. *Bilge-water ; the lowest of the people, rabble ; mob.*

sentĭo, sensi, sensum, sentire, a. *To feel, see ; to perceive.*

sequor, sěcūtus sum, sěqui, dep. *To follow ; to comply with, conform to.*

sermo, ōnis, m. *A speaking ; talk, conversation.*

sēr-ō, adv. (ser-us) *Late, too late.*

serv-ĭo, ĭvi, ĭtum, ire, n. (serv-us) *To be a slave ; to serve.*

servo, āvi, ātum, āre, a. *To save, preserve, protect.*

servus, i, m. *A slave.*

sēsē, reduplicated form of acc. or abl. of sui.

sěvēr-ĭtas, ātis, f. (severus) *Strictness, severity.*

sex-tus, a, um, ord. num. adj. (sex) *The sixth.*

si, conj. *If, whether.*

sīc, adv. *In this manner, so thus.*

sīca, ae, f. *A dagger, poniard.*

sīc-ut or sic-uti, adv. *So as, just as.*

silent-ĭum, ii, n. (silens, *silent*) *Silence.*

sĭlěo, ui, no sup., n. *To be noiseless, still, or silent.*

sĭmĭlis, e, adj. (with gen. and dat.) *Like, similar.*

sĭmul, adv. *Together, at once ;* simul-ac or atque, *as soon as.*

sī-n, conj. (si ; ne) *But if.*

sine, prep. with abl. *Without.*

singŭli, ae, a, num. distrib. adj. *One to each, separate, single, each, every.*

sĭno, sĭvi, sĭtum, sinĕre, a. *To let, suffer, allow.*

sŏcĭ-etas, ātis, f. (soci-us) *Fellowship, association, society ; a league, an alliance.*

socius, ii, m. *A partner, companion ; ally, confederate.*

sŏdālis, is, com. gen. *A boon companion.*

sŏlĕo, sŏlĭtus sum; n. semi-dep. *To be wont, be accustomed.*

sōl-ĭtūdo, ĭnis, f. (sol-us) *Loneliness, solitude ; a desert, wilderness.*

sōl-um, adv. (sōl-us) *Alone, only.*

somnus, i, m. *Sleep, slumber.*

spěcŭl-or, dep. a. and n. (specula, *a watch-tower*) *To watch, observe, explore.*

spe-s, spěi, f., gen., dat., and abl. pl. not found in good writers (for sper-s, fr. spěr-o) *Hope.*

spir-ĭtus, ūs, m. (spir-o) *A breathing; a breath.*

spon-te, abl., and spontis, gen. of the noun spons, f. (for spond-te, fr. spond-eo, *to pledge*) *Of one's own accord, willingly.*

stā-tor, ōris, m. *A supporter, stayer.*

stătŭ-o, ui, ūtum, ĕre, a. (status) *To put, place; to decide, determine.*

stā-tus, ūs, m. (sto) *Condition, situation, state.*

stirps, stirpis, f. *A stock, stem; source, origin.*

sto, stĕti, stātum, stāre, n. *To stand.*

stŭdĕo, ūi, no sup., ēre, n. and a. *To be eager; to pursue, be devoted to.*

stŭd-ĭum, ii, n. (stud-eo) *Assiduity, zeal.*

stultus, a, um, adj. *Foolish, simple.*

stuprum, i (u long or short), n. *Debauchery, lewdness.*

suādeo, suāsi, suāsum, suādēre, n. and a. *To advise, recommend.*

sub-sell-ĭum, ii, n. (sub; sell-a) *A bench, judge's seat.*

sŭi, sibi, se or sese, pron. reflex. *Of himself, herself, itself, or themselves.*

sum, esse, fūi, no sup., n. irr. *Te be, exist.*

summus, a, um, sup. adj. (superus) *The highest, greatest, very great; the most important; the top of, the summit of.*

sŭpĕr-ĭor, ĭus, comp. adj. (super) *Higher; earlier, former.*

supplĭc-ĭum, ii, n. (supplic-o) *A humble petition; punishment.*

sus-cĭpĭo, cēpi, ceptum, cĭpĕre, a. *To undertake.*

suspec-tus, a, um, part. (suspic-io, through true root suspec) *Mistrusted, suspected.*

su-spĭcĭo, spexi, spectum, spĭcĕre, a. and n. (sub; specio, *to look*) *To look at from under; to mistrust, suspect.*

suspĭc-ĭo, ōnis, f. (suspĭc-or) *Mistrust, suspicion.*

suspĭc-or, ātus, sum, āri, dep (suspĭc-io) *To suspect.*

suspitio: see suspicio.

sus-tĭneo, tĭnūi, tentum, tĭnēre, a. *To support, sustain.*

sŭ-us, a, um, poss. pron. (su-i) *Of or belonging to himself, herself, itself, or themselves; his own, her own, its own, their own.*

T .

tăbŭla, ae, f. *A board; a writing-tablet.*

tăcĕo, ŭi, ĭtum, n. *To be silent.*

tăcĭturn-ĭtas, ātis, tăcēre, f. (taciturnus, *quiet*) *Silence.*

tăc-ĭtus, a, um, adj. (taceo) *Silent.*

tae-ter, tra, trum, adj. (for taedter, fr. taed-et) *Foul, shameful, disgraceful.*

tam, adv. *So, so far, so very, so much.*

tămen, adv. *Nevertheless, however, still.*

tăm-etsi, conj. (contracted fr. tamen-etsi) *Although, though.*

tan-dem, adv. (tam) *At length; in questions, pray.*

tam-quam, adv. (tam ; quam) *As much as; just as, like as, as if, as it were.*

tantus, a, um, adj. *So great, so large, so many.*

tec-tum, i, n. (for teg-tum, fr. teg-o) *A roof, house.*

tēlum, i, n. *A spear; weapon.*

tempes-tas, ātis, f. (for temportas, fr. tempus) *A space of time; a time; weather (both good and bad), hence a storm, tempest.*

templum, i, n. *A temple, shrine.*

temp-to, tāvi, tātum, tāre, a. intens. (also written ten-td, fr. ten-eo) *To handle; to try; to try the strength of; to attack.*

tempus, ŏris, n. *A portion of time; a time; a critical moment, circumstances.*

tĕnĕbrae, ārum, f. pl. *Darkness.*

těnĕo, těnŭi, tentum, a., těnĕre.
To hold, keep, have, guard.

terra. ae, f. *The earth, land ;
orbis terrarum, the world ; country.*

tĭmĕo, ŭi, no sup., tĭnĕre, a. and
n. *To fear.*

tĭm-or, ŏris, m. *Fear.*

tollo, sustŭli, sublātum, tollĕre,
a. *To lift up ; to destroy, take away.*

tot, num. adj. indecl. *So many.*

tŏt-ĭes, (iens) num. adv. (tot) *So
often, so many times.*

tōtus, a, um, adj. *All, all the ;
the whole ; in adverbial force, altogether, wholly.*

trans-fĕro, ferre, tŭli, lātum, a.
*To bear across ; to transport, trans-
fer.*

tribŭn-al, ālis, n. (tribunus) *A
judgment-seat, tribunal.*

trib-ŭnus, i, m. (trib-us) *A
tribune.*

tru-cĭdo, a. (for truc-caedo, fr.
trux [savage] ; caedo) *To slaughter.*

tū, tui, pers. pron. *Thou, you
(sing.)*

tum, adv. *Then, at that time.*

tŭmultus, ūs, m. *Disturbance,
tumult.*

turp-ĭtŭdo, inis, f. (turpis) *Base-
ness, infamy.*

tū-tus, a, um, (tu-eor) *Safe,
secure.*

tŭ-us, a, um, poss. pron. (tu)
Thy, thine, your, yours.

U

ŭbi, adv. (akin to qui) *Where ;
when ; ubinam, where, pray?*

ul-lus, a, um, adj. dim. (for un-
lus, fr. unus) *Any, any one.*

umquam : see unquam.

ūnā, adv. (adverbial abl. of unus)
*At the same time, in company, to-
gether.*

V

vir-tus, ūtis, f. (vir) *Manliness,
manhood ; courage ; worth, merit.*

vis, vis, f. *Strength, force.*

viscus, ĕris, n. (mostly in pl.)
The inwards ; the viscera.

vĭ-ta, ae, f. (for viv-ta, fr. viv-o)
Life.

vĭtĭum, ii, n. *Fault, blemish,
error, crime, vice.*

vĭto, āvi, ātum, āre, a. *To shun,
avoid.*

vīvo, vixi, victum, vīvĕre, n. *To
live.*

vīv-us, a, um, adj. (vĭv-o) *Alive.*

vix, adv. *With difficulty, hardly,
scarcely ; vixdum, scarcely.*

vŏco, āvi, ātum, āre, a. *To call ;
summon.*

volnĕr-o, āvi, ātissu, āre, a.
(volnus) *To wound.*

volo, velle, volŭi, no sup., a. irr.
To will, wish, desire.

voltus : see vultus.

volun-tas, ātis, f. (for volent-
tas, fr. volens) *Will, wish, desire,
inclination.*

volup-tas, ātis, f. (volup, agreeable) *Enjoyment, pleasure, delight.*

vox, vōcis, f. (for voc-s, fr. voc-o,
*that which calls out) A voice ; a
word ; in pl., language, sayings,
words.*

vul-tus, ūs, m. (for vol-tus, fr.
vol-o) *The countenance ; looks, as-
pect.*

THE COPP CLARK COMPANY, LIMITED, PRINTERS, COLBORNE STREET.

CPSIA information can be obtained
at www.ICGtesting.com
Printed in the USA
BVHW031939190622
639865BV00010B/243